CH00323700

Acknowledgements

I should like to thank the following for their help in the preparation of this book: Sue Bond, Heather McConnell, Peter Cheek, Ronald Cook, Dan Klein, Maureen Thompson, David Black, Denzil and Nicky Grant, Anne and Trevor Martin, and Michael Wisehall.

Noël Riley

August 1986

Contents

Introduction

This book is intended for existing or would-be professionals, earning their living by working full time in the antiques trade, whether from a shop, from home, from a market stall or in a combination of ways.

The term 'antique' is technically defined in most quarters as anything over 100 years old, and this is applied for such purposes as Customs and Excise and in the vetting systems of many fairs. At the same time, people have come to recognise that the creation of works of art did not end with the nineteenth century and that many more recent items are highly collectable. So the 'antiques trade', for the purposes of this book, must embrace not only businesses concerned with genuine antiques as defined by the 100-year rule, but also the ever-increasing range of collectable goods, from Edwardian paintings to 1930s ceramics and post-war Dinky toys, through which dealers can earn their livings.

Whether one likes it or not, in talking of the antiques trade, particularly with regard to furniture, one is also including a great many dealers in spurious or 'made up' items which may be passed off as antiques. Whether these people find much satisfaction in their profession is open to question, but without doubt many of them make a good deal of money.

Antiques has, in a general way, become an umbrella term which embraces practically any collectable item. To major categories like pictures, sculpture, furniture, ceramics and glass, silver and metalwork, textiles, jewellery, books and oriental works of art have been added newer subjects of interest such as early photographs and photographic equipment, scientific and mechanical instruments, packaging and printed ephemera, agricultural implements, domestic utensils, tools, toys and tribal art. Even juke boxes are now sold in the fine art auction rooms: computer games may follow in years to come.

The trade

The antiques trade in Britain probably comprises more than 10,000 businesses, involving as many as 20,000 individuals. Another 2000 to 3000 people are employed in antique and chattel auctioneering, but their enterprises are not our chief concern in this book. Antique dealers range from those with luxurious premises in the Bond Street or Belgravia areas of London, and with annual turnovers of hundreds of thousands of pounds, to market stall-holders scratching a living by relying on a rapid turnover of goods at low prices. In between these extremes lie the vast majority of *bona fide* antique dealers who run businesses of widely varying sizes and sorts up and down the country. The greatest concentration of them is, of course, in London, where it is estimated that about 3000 to 4000 dealers operate.

London's dealers include some of the most prestigious in the world, catering for the very rich international retail market in top quality furniture, pictures and works of art of all kinds. But these only represent the tip of a huge pyramid comprising hundreds of other antiques businesses in the capital, dealing with both retail and trade buyers from all over the world. At the base of the pyramid are the vast numbers of stall-holders working the wide range of markets— both full and part time—where collectors and dealers constantly swarm in search of bargains. These include indoor markets such as Gray's, off Oxford Street, and Antiquarius in the King's Road, as well as famous open-air once-weekly markets like Portobello Road (Saturday), Bermondsey (Friday) and Brick Lane (Sunday). Whole districts like Camden Passage in Islington and the Church Street area of Paddington are given over to a mixture of antique and *bric-à-brac* shops and open-air stalls until it sometimes seems that the entire world is either buying or selling the past.

While in London may be found the greatest concentration of antique dealers anywhere, there is hardly a village left in Britain which cannot boast at least one junk shop, and many small towns offer a range of businesses from the rarefied and expensive to *bric-à-brac* stalls in the weekly market: many cities have their own regular antiques markets, one or two days a week if not full time, and in others there are periodic fairs which attract buyers from a wide area.

Fairs include up-market events where the quality and authenticity of the goods on sale are guaranteed by vetting systems; some of these continue for a week or more and others for two or three days. At the other end of the scale are the one- and two-day *bric-à-brac* and collectors' fairs which have no datelines or restrictions as to what may be sold.

Professional organisations

About 430 well-established dealers from all over Britain belong to the British Antique Dealers' Association (BADA), founded in 1918 to 'watch over and protect the interests of the Trade as a whole'. Its members are expected to maintain the highest standards of integrity and knowledge, and thus 'enhance the standing of the Trade and engender a spirit of confidence in the collecting world'. Joining the BADA involves a lengthy process of recommendation and inspection by existing members; acceptance of a new member is based on a dealer's reputation for honest dealing, expert knowledge and high quality stock; a dealer's membership is reviewed every year.

The BADA not only provides a professional body for the upper echelons of the antiques trade, but it undertakes a number of functions connected with it. It was the BADA that first negotiated the agreements with certain foreign governments by which they accept goods over 100 years old free of import duty, and its members are called upon to 'vet' goods being shipped abroad to determine whether they are dutiable or not, in other words, whether they are 100 years old or more. Furthermore, representatives of the Association regularly act in an advisory capacity on the export of works of art (see page 91) and are sometimes called upon to arbitrate in disputes between antique dealers or dealers and customers, in many cases obviating the need for legal proceedings. The BADA helps to organise the Grosvenor House Antiques and the North of England Antiques Fair at Harrogate, while participants in the West of England Antiques Fair at Bath must be BADA members. The Association runs training courses in antique restoration at West Dean College in Sussex. Affiliated to the International Confederation of Art Dealers (CINOA) it also promotes the British antiques trade in many other, less tangible, ways.

The Society of London Art Dealers (SLAD) is a similar body to the BADA concerned with picture dealers and dealing, and the Antiquarian Booksellers Association (ABA) with the antiquarian book trade.

In 1974 the London and Provincial Antique Dealers' Association (LAPADA) was formed. This is now a widely respected professional body comprising nearly 700 dealers, shipping and packing agents, restorers and valuers from all over the country. Membership is open to traders of not less than three years' experience who are registered for VAT and who are 'able to satisfy the membership committee that they have the necessary integrity, stock and knowledge...'. The organisation strives to maintain standards of integrity and honest dealing in a similar way to the other organisations.

Many antique dealers belong to regional groups such as the Cotswold Antique Dealers' Association, the Perthshire Antique Dealers' Association or the New Forest Antique Dealers' Association, which can be helpful both in promoting their combined interests and in maintaining standards for members. While many extremely good and honest dealers belong to no professional bodies or organisations, these are a form of safeguard for the public, providing some sort of system of redress for dissatisfied customers, and in their implication of both high standards of goods and fair dealing, they engender a confidence that is extremely valuable to many dealers.

What it takes

Many people imagine that antique dealing is an easy option and the quickest way to a fast buck. They hear stories of lucky 'finds', bought for a song and sold for huge profits, and forget that most people (and antique dealers are no exception) are more willing to discuss their successes than their mistakes. It seems that all you have to do is find a pitch, gather together enough goods to fill it, and the world will come running to make you rich. Anyone who has tried to earn a living (and not just a little pin-money) from antiques or *bric-à-brac* will tell you that this is far from the reality.

Dealing is a strenuous occupation, requiring total dedication, iron nerves, at least a modicum of expertise, some capital and a good deal of luck. It normally involves travelling long distances, much lifting and shifting of goods, and a deal of risk. A dealer must have courage (and capital) to back his judgements when he is buying, and as practically everything he buys will have to be assessed individually, he must have knowledge. He must be prepared to face disappointments and quiet periods when nothing seems to be happening and business looks doomed.

On the bright side, however, is the fact that antique dealing offers an endlessly varied career, with more than a fair share of interest and excitement and at least the possibility of making a good living.

Of all the qualities needed by the antique dealer, that combination of informed observation and visual memory known as a 'good eye' is probably the most important. Some people seem to be born with it and others manage to cultivate it, but there are those who, however much they read, however hard they look, however often they touch and however assiduously they learn, never manage to acquire this elusive magic ingredient which seems to separate the good dealers from the mediocre.

Enthusiasm and the ability to work hard go hand in hand, and these are vital to the success of any antique dealing venture. Many dealers think little of driving 300 or 400 miles in a day in search of stock or to visit an auction; depending on their specialisation, they are likely to have to lift heavy loads, of furniture or books for example, with backaching frequency. They may have to visit private houses to view property—for sale or valuation—at short notice; they must be continuously alive to possible sources of stock, and all this time there is probably a shop or gallery to organise. Antique dealing is not for those who like predictable routine and predetermined hours of work.

A good business sense is another important attribute—if you have not got it yourself, find a reliable partner who has, and be guided by him or her. You may have the eye and the knowledge, and even the selling ability, but without proper financial management these can easily fail.

Why be a dealer?

People take up antique dealing professionally, that is to say, as their main means of livelihood, for multitudes of reasons. There are those for whom there simply is not and never was any other career. Some of these come from well-established antique-dealing families and have art and antiques as well as the dealer's instincts in their bones. While they may be lucky in having a ready-made business to go into, at the same time they will almost certainly have their eyes open to the risks and hard work involved, and few dealers will take on even their own sons and daughters unless they are prepared to gain knowledge and experience, either elsewhere or by working in a menial capacity for a number of years before progressing to a responsible position in the business.

Numbers of people decide at a young age that a career in antiques is for them, and these have to be single-minded in pursuit of their goal. In an oversubscribed profession, it is often extremely difficult to find an opening, and only the most dedicated—or the very lucky—will succeed.

One of the most widely accepted routes to dealing is to work as an assistant in an antique shop. This provides valuable practice in dealing with customers as well as opportunities to learn, but it does not give the most important experience of all, which is to buy, since few dealers trust their assistants to spend money on their behalf. Some give them the chance to view sales for them and to undertake projects of research, perhaps in a museum, and in rare cases may take them on buying or valuing trips—all extremely useful ways to gain knowledge—but on the whole, a dealer's assistant is there to manage the shop or gallery, and as the boss is likely to be out buying for much of the time, it can be a job of considerable responsibility.

Working as a dealer's assistant is, however, an excellent way to learn about the trade and to discover whether or not you have a natural ability to sell—a flair which is obviously of inestimable value when it comes to dealing on your own account. How much you will learn will depend a good deal on your own attitude. Most dealers like to have knowledgeable and interested helpers and will welcome your questions. Many keep selections of reference books relating to the kinds of stock in which they specialise and time spent studying these is well worth while. The more background knowledge you can acquire the more you have to build on, and the more you will probably find your boss is prepared to impart information.

While it is often difficult to find a job with an antique dealer, and you cannot afford to be too choosy, it is clearly important to avoid working with someone whose taste and interests differ too widely from your own. On the other hand, it is not always essential to find a specialist dealer in the kinds of antiques you hope to pursue later. A good general dealer will give you a solid grounding in all kinds of areas and may even fire your enthusiasm for a speciality you had not discovered before; furthermore, a background in other kinds of antiques may prove useful for a specialist later. Unless you are totally committed to a particular avenue of specialisation, such as oriental works of art, ceramics, carpets and so on, it is probably more useful to attach yourself to a dealer with a fairly general stock to begin with. Later you may decide to gain more specialised knowledge by working for another dealer, or you may find yourself confident enough to go it alone.

Another well-trodden path into antique dealing is to be found in the saleroom. It is in Britain's auction rooms that the greatest variety of antiques and *bric-à-brac* can be experienced, and training in the auctioneering profession provides an excellent all-round knowledge for any would-be dealer. While the majority of young people lucky enough to find training posts in the salerooms tend to remain in the auction world, some do move into dealing on their own account, either sooner or later.

The collector as dealer

Some dealers begin their careers as collectors. Many of these are specialists who become deeply interested in a particular aspect of antiques, their knowledge grows, and they eventually realise that they can capitalise on years of experience and involvement. Their specialist knowledge of their chosen subject is likely to place them at a great advantage, but buying for a collection and buying to resell are two different things, and commercial considerations have to come first for the dealer. This transition, from collector to dealer, is not always easy.

While some collectors become dealers, there are few dealers who are not also collectors. They may simply be interested in furnishing their homes with antiques of the highest quality, or they may collect in a purely speculative way, focusing on some field which they consider under-valued, with a view to selling at some time in the future when, they hope, their collection has become much more valuable. Others, probably the majority, are dealer-collectors who regard dealing as much a means of adding to their collection as a way of earning a living. Indeed, some find it hard to make much of a living: magpie-like, they cannot resist keeping their best finds, whether they can really afford to or not. These sorts of antique dealers, imbued as they usually are with a genuine feeling for the goods they have rather than a concern to make money out of them, are often the most interesting to meet and deal with. They enjoy discussion, are willing to share their knowledge and like to regard their customers as fellow enthusiasts.

Linked with the collecting instinct of many dealers is the thirst for knowledge that leads many into the trade. There are few careers which can rival antique dealing for the sheer opportunity to learn. Hardly a day will go past in a dealer's life when he will not have seen or discovered something new to him, and this is one of the most enticing aspects of it. 'Never seen one like it before' is a phrase often heard among dealers, and it is one that signals a characteristic excitement.

Change of direction

A large number of people faced with redundancy, retirement and other changes in their lives consider antique dealing as a potentially interesting and lucrative way of life. Actors with long 'resting' periods, or dancers, customarily obliged to retire young, are among those who have turned to antiques for a new career, some with eminent success. Dentists, accountants, engineers and teachers are among the many other professionals who have become antique dealers in mid-career.

Those with good redundancy payments, golden handshakes or other sources of capital are obviously advantaged in these circumstances, but anyone thinking about embarking on an antique dealing business should consider the financial aspects very carefully. Knowledge is, of course, the other essential ingredient for success, and those with many years of collecting behind them are likely to be well equipped.

Gathering experience

It is unusual and certainly unwise for anyone to set up his or her own antiques business 'cold', that is to say, without previous experience working for someone else, as a collector, or in a small way on one's own behalf. One-day fairs can be an excellent introduction to dealing: gathering together enough stock to fill a trestle table and then trying to sell it for a profit should give the novice an insight into the difficulties involved without costing too much precious capital.

Fairs will also reveal sales talent. This may be less important than many people imagine: 'the right goods sell themselves' is the belief of many, and aggressive selling is not always appropriate. On the other hand, a visit to any busy *bric-à-brac* market leaves one in no doubt that a flair for selling can make up for all kinds of shortcomings in the goods on offer. 'You'll be sure to have company tonight' went the cheerful sales patter of a seller of second-hand put-U-up beds in the 1930s. His customers may not have bothered to imagine what sort of company he meant, for they willingly bought his beds.

A stall in the local town market may be a useful beginning. This would be a more regular commitment than the occasional one-day fair, and it is not always fun to stand about in the wet and the cold wondering if you'll make enough profit to pay the rent, but you'll learn a good deal about what sells and what doesn't, and you'll almost certainly make useful contacts. Information about the setting up of market stalls should be available from the local town council. The cost generally depends on the footage of your pitch, but usually works out at about £10 or a little less for a day's trading.

To specialise or diversify

Some people are natural magpies and find themselves unable to specialise. They find too much of interest to concentrate on any one kind of item and prefer to explore a wide area. These will build up a wide general knowledge, probably with deeper experience in some fields than others, and perhaps some pockets of admitted total ignorance. Others find satisfaction in detailed knowledge and expertise within a limited field. Specialisation can certainly lead to a much deeper understanding of a particular subject, and may give a level of expertise that is most rewarding.

It is probably a good idea not to commit yourself to a speciality to begin with, but to deal in a fairly general range until you have a good idea of what is and is not 'commercial', and until you have acquired a sound all-round knowledge. Many dealers also maintain that it is not so easy to specialise successfully in country areas. Some who have become well-established specialists in London have found that on moving to the country they need to carry a more wide-ranging stock if they are to attract local clients. One way to get over this is to deal in a general way from a shop, and indulge in the specialised goods at occasional fairs.

Above all, whether you deal as a specialist or in the most general way, remember that it is easier to sell things that you yourself like. Buying goods with which you feel no affinity, for purely commercial reasons, is likely to be demoralising and surprisingly uncommercial. The chances are that if you do not particularly enjoy looking at or living with an object, other people will feel the same, and it will become a 'sticker'.

Gaining background knowledge

It is unlikely that anyone using this book will be starting their career in antiques from scratch: even if they have not run a business before, their interest in antiques will probably have been exercised in one way or another. They may have had experience in one-day fairs, with regular market stalls or as collectors.

However, they may still feel a need to 'bone up' and perhaps gain a stronger general grounding of knowledge, and there is a variety of possibilities from university degrees to 'do-it-yourself' disciplines (see page 130). There are also a number of privately run courses which provide a study of historical styles and streams, and give detailed teaching on the decorative arts. While they do not profess to give a complete preparation for running an antiques business they can give a valuable all-round basis on which to build specialised knowledge. After all, as a dealer you will continue to learn all your life, but a broad general knowledge to start with will enable you to make the most of your later experience.

University courses can be enticing for those of a

studious inclination, and a few are now devoted to the decorative arts, whereas until a few years ago the fine arts were an exclusive focus. Several history of art courses are now usefully combined with languages and some are of a more practical nature than others. However, while one or two are designed especially for those bent on a career in museums, there is no university course specifically intended for would-be antique dealers and three or four years spent gaining background which is inevitably only theoretical might be regarded as somewhat self-indulgent.

While university degree courses are lengthy and not always relevant, however enjoyable, and the privately run fine and decorative arts courses tend to be expensive, there is nothing to stop the self-disciplined enthusiast from pursuing his or her own course of intensive study.

There are many hundreds of books on antiques and, although many have little value as reference books, there are plenty of well-researched and authoritative works which are worth studying. If you can afford to buy a few carefully chosen definitive works on different aspects of antiques, the outlay will almost certainly prove a good investment. Public libraries are usually helpful in procuring from other sources any books they do not have in stock, and for those in London, specialist art publications are available for reference in Westminster City Library and the National Art Library at the Victoria and Albert Museum. Unlike the British Library and some others, you do not need a special permit to visit them.

Reading as much as possible should form the basis of a DIY course; visits to museums and country houses and careful viewing of the best examples in any field will help to inform your eye, guide your sense of proportion, reinforce what you have read, and give you a yardstick of quality. Some people find that sketching objects in museums and houses helps to focus their visual study, and it is certainly a good idea to concentrate on a few items rather than take a cursory glance at hundreds. Lectures and gallery talks in museums, adult education classes and other lecture courses can be excellent and many are inexpensive if not completely free (those in the national museums, for example); if they are available to you, don't miss the opportunity to gain from them.

The next step in the DIY antiques course is to spend time going round the trade even though you may have no intention of spending money at this stage. Auctions provide a very satisfactory means of study: viewing sessions allow you to look at and handle goods in conjunction with the catalogue descriptions, and attendance at the sale itself will give insights into the commercial side. Visiting dealers and talking to them can also be most informative. You will soon discover which are the most knowledgeable and enthusiastic and which enjoy discussing their stock. Many welcome questions and like an opportunity to talk even if they do not make a sale at this stage.

Chapter 1
Opening a Business

To a great many people setting up in business is synonymous with establishing a limited company. It brings with it visions of favourable tax treatment, bank managers rushing to lend money and suppliers willing to extend credit. If that was ever the case, it is no longer so. In many ways a self-employed person is better off in terms of allowances than one who is the employee of his own company—for that is your status as a working shareholder, as we shall shortly explain. As far as loans or credit are concerned, the failure rate among new small businesses—limited companies as much as other trading entities—has caused banks and experienced suppliers to treat them all the same way: with caution.

That incidentally, is a course of action we also recommend to you in the course of running your business. It is extremely unwise to let anyone take goods out of your premises on the undertaking that they 'will pay later'. Sadly, that applies to good friends and valued customers as well as to strangers. It also applies to payments by cheque. They should be cleared with the bank before you part with the goods.

Limited companies

The reason why the owners of a limited company are treated as employees from a tax point of view if they also work in it is that, in law, a company has an identity that is quite separate from its shareholders. This means that if the company goes out of business, the creditors' claims are limited to the assets of the company which include any capital *issued* to the shareholders—that is, the money they have put into it. Their personal assets cannot be touched.

There is a big difference between *issued* and *authorised* or *nominal* share capital. It is perfectly possible to have a company with an authorised capital running into five or even six figures, but for the issued capital to be £100 or less. From the point of view of the credibility of any company to whom you are supplying goods, the only figure that means anything is the issued capital. The only liability over and above that and the company's assets arises if they have been trading fraudulently: buying goods in the knowledge that they cannot pay for them.

There are obvious advantages in trading as a limited company if you are buying your stock on credit. It enables you to fill your shelves secure in the knowledge that if they fail to sell and you are unable to meet your obligations, your personal assets cannot be touched. For instance, if you begin your business by printing 10,000 copies of a booklet describing your activities and running up a print bill of £2000 to £3000 you might be well advised to opt for limited company status.

Furthermore, the legal requirements of operating as a limited company are fairly onerous. Among other things, you have to file annual audited accounts with the Registrar of Companies and observe certain formalities in the way you run your business which, though routine to those used to them, are fairly complicated for the uninitiated. You can, of course, get your accountant or solicitor to handle them for you, but that costs money. Furthermore you will have to know at least the elements of what is involved yourself, since the responsibility is ultimately yours, not that of any third party who is acting for you.

Sole traders

The principal point to remember about operating as a sole trader is that you are personally liable for the debts of the business. You might think that is a disadvantage when it comes to borrowing money, but in fact the banks are very canny about lending money to limited companies because they know that in theory their limited liability status would make it virtually impossible to recover any loan, should the business fail. The banks therefore treat limited companies in exactly the same way as they would treat a sole trader or indeed a private individual. They ask for a *personal* guarantee which, in the case of a company, overrides its limited status; unless, of course, its issued share capital and assets are large enough to give full security to the loan.

There is, therefore, no disadvantage in operating as a sole trader from the point of view of finance, though it underlines the importance of buying within the limits of what you can afford. In terms of tax, there are certain advantages in operating as a sole trader. If you have been an employee previously, paying tax on a PAYE basis, you can offset losses in the first four years of trading against tax previously paid and get it back. Losses made by a company can only be set off against the company's subsequent profits, not against the tax of the individual shareholders. Even if they invest their own money in it and lose it, they can only set the loss off against capital gains, not against income tax.

Furthermore, the tax allowances against earnings of a self-employed person or sole trader are much more favourable than those available to people taxed on a PAYE basis—and that is how you would be taxed as a director/shareholder of your own company because, remember, the company is a separate entity from you as an individual. You can, of course, charge a good deal 'to the company' but the advantages of doing so have been somewhat eroded since the rate of corporation tax on small companies (those with annual profits of less than £100,000) was reduced to 30 per cent, the same as the standard rate of income tax.

In essence, any expenditure 'wholly and exclusively incurred for the purposes of business' can be charged against earnings by a sole trader in making his or her tax return. That covers not only goods bought for resale or for use in the business, and services like postage, telephone, gas and electricity, but travel, insurance, hotel bills and also:

- Carriage, packing and delivery costs;
- Wages and salaries paid to employees;
- Interest on business loans;
- The running expenses of your car when used for business;
- Legal and professional fees;
- Meals when travelling on business;
- Periodicals and books bought on business;
- Subscriptions to trade or professional bodies.

The essential point here, of course, is to keep as many bills as possible to substantiate your claims and also to keep a book in which you regularly, preferably daily, record sales and business purchases. Your accountant will advise you of the records he or she wants you to keep—the requirements may differ slightly according to the exact nature of your business and your accountant's own preferences; for instance, he may want you to provide analysis columns in which expenditure and income is categorised to make the task of preparing the tax return somewhat easier. But as a sole trader, you will not have to produce audited accounts in the way a limited company has to; nor do you have to keep minutes of directors' meetings, have a registered office, or go through the various bits of corporate rigmarole that are required by law of such trading entities.

Partnerships

The nature of antique dealing, which often requires a responsible person to be on the premises while another is buying, or where two heads are better than one in making buying decisions, often means that they are established as partnerships. Partnerships, in fact, are a way of setting up a business with one or more other people that avoids most of the administrative headaches of doing this by forming a limited company. But you do not have the protection of limited liability either. A partnership is treated in law in exactly the same way as a sole trader, with the further potential disadvantage that all the members of a partnership are personally liable for its debts, even if these are incurred by a piece of mismanagement or some other act by any one partner that was not known to the others. So the choice of partners is a step that requires very careful thought. Certainly, you should not bring in a partner just for the sake of having company, because unless the partner really can contribute something to the business—either money or essential expertise—you are giving away a part of what, in time, could be a valuable asset to little purpose. You might, in fact, be better advised to have that person as a paid employee, if the main purpose of having him or her work with you is to help out.

But whatever the reason for establishing a partnership, as opposed to going it alone and owning the whole business, you should be sure that the person is someone you know really well. (There can, of course, be more than one partner.) A lot of partnerships come adrift because the partners find themselves incompatible, because their ideas about running the business differ, or because one of them does not pull his or her weight. Breaking up a partnership in such circumstances can be filled with hideously expensive legal complications and for this reason, it is essential that a deed of partnership is drawn up by a solicitor before you even start. It should cover such points as:

- Who is responsible for what aspects of running the business?
- How are profits divided?
- What items of expenditure can be charged to the partnership?
- If one of the partners dies or withdraws, how is their share of the business to be divided?
- What arbitration arrangements are there, in case of irreconcilable differences?

Business names

One thing all these forms of business have in common is that they have to follow the provisions relating to the use of business names. If you trade under any name other than your own, or, in the case of a partnership, the names of the partners, you must show the names and business addresses of all the owners on:

    business letters

    written orders for the supply of goods and
      services

    invoices and receipts issued in the course of
      business

    written demands for payment.

Furthermore you have to display this information prominently on your premises. If you are trading as a limited company you also have to show its registration number, the names of the directors, and the address of its registered office on letterheads and any catalogues you might issue. At one time all these details had to be organised through the Registrar of Business Names but it is now left to the individual firm. However, the penalties for not complying with these provisions are quite severe and it is absolutely vital to make sure that you do so on all your printed matter.

Buying an existing business

Shops are generally leasehold and the first thing you should look at is the length of the lease and the conditions for renewal if there is a review clause after a certain period of time—there generally is. The crucial point is obviously whether there is any ceiling to the amount by which the landlord can raise the rent. Apart from the tenancy, though, you will be buying the stock, fixtures and fittings and the goodwill.

Buying the stock in an antique shop is particularly tricky because, unlike new goods, the market value is not clear cut. Even the record of what the owner paid for them, though this helps, is not an infallible indication that they can be sold at that price. The goods may also need to be inspected for damage, certainly in the case of the more valuable items. Buying existing stock, in fact, should be subject to a very careful inspection and, possibly, an independent valuation. Fixtures and fittings should also be valued independently.

'Goodwill' is a nebulous concept to which an exact value cannot be attached, certainly in the case of a shop relying on passing trade. Much more relevant is the accessibility of the premises, whether you can get larger items through the doors, whether the character of the neighbourhood 'feels right' in terms of the sort of business you are intending to transact and whether it has a good record for security and freedom from crime.

A further point that needs to be checked is whether the owner has kept any accounts to support his claims regarding the value of the business. Interpreting accounts can be a tricky matter; for instance, the owner may claim that he has understated his or her profits to reduce the tax liability. Whatever documentation is produced, it should be looked at by an accountant. Other terms and conditions will have to be vetted by your solicitor.

Chapter 2
Raising Capital

Because a lot of people start out in the antique trade by selling off parts of their own collection — generally items acquired cheaply over a period of years — they tend to underestimate the amount of capital that is required to turn a hobby into a business. The initial stock has to be sold at prices high enough to enable it to be replaced and getting prices right is a somewhat inexact science in the antique business.

It can be a matter of fashion. A few years ago nobody placed much value on early photographs and they could be bought literally for pennies. Much the same was true for nineteenth-century studio pots or eighteenth-century blue and white earthenware. Now they go for very high prices and if you had bought them when they were cheap you might not realise how much you could get for them or how expensive they could be to replace. On the other hand, there are items like Stevengraphs that were very popular in the sixties but which are less highly regarded now. It is, on the whole, easier to sell than to buy, but everyone gets landed with a 'sticker' now and then; nor can you guarantee that even a high quality, high priced item will sell quickly.

You need money for other purposes, of course, as well as stock. There are all the costs of running the business: rent, rates, telephone, light, heat, postage and travel to mention just a few. You will want to pay yourself a wage and you will have to pay staff if you have people helping you. If your turnover is over £20,500 a year you will have to register for VAT and pay that quarterly on your sales or in the case of the special scheme (see pages 89-90) on the difference between purchase and selling price; and if you are making profits, you will have to pay tax. All these

Running Your Own Antiques Business

obligations will have to be met in cash. If you do not
have the cash you would be forced to try and sell
goods in the shop at what, in such circumstances,
could be less than market rates. For this reason it is
essential that you spend some time making a realistic
assessment of how much money you need, preferably
with the help of your accountant, and making arrangements to borrow money to cover any shortfalls that
might occur. It is always easier to borrow money
before you actually need it than when the creditors
are pounding at your door. Lenders become notice-
ably less enthusiastic under these circumstances.

With the boom in small business and the govern-
ment's encouragement of them, a considerable number of potential sources of finance have sprung up.
One that is not actually a means of funding a business but that could be very useful in supplementing
your own income if you have been drawing unemploy-
ment or supplementary benefit for eight weeks and
have £1000 of your own money to invest in your business (it can be a loan from someone else) is the *Enterprise Allowance*. Awarded at the discretion of your
local Jobcentre, it gives you £40 a week for the first
52 weeks that you are in business. You must, however, apply for the Enterprise Allowance *before* you
start trading. It will not be granted once you have
already begun operations. But at the risk of making
the kind of categorical statement that someone is
almost bound to find an exception to, none of the
actual funding schemes (through merchant banks
and other sources of venture capital) is applicable to
an antiques business. For this, and for most other
forms of small business, the only outside source of
finance, apart from personal loans, is through the
banks.

Money from the banks

The commonest form of help, as far as small businesses are concerned, is an overdraft facility. You
will be given facilities to overdraw up to a certain
amount, but the advantage of an overdraft, as
opposed to a loan, is that interest (usually 2 to 3 per

cent above base lending rate) is paid only on the actual amount by which you are overdrawn. Overdrafts are particularly useful, therefore, for the firm whose pattern of business fluctuates, and an antiques business, occasionally buying a high priced item, comes into that category. The disadvantage of an overdraft is that it can be called in. Though in practice this rarely happens, it is unwise to use money raised in this way to finance medium- and long-term requirements, particularly those which make no immediate contribution to profits, like buying a smart new van. A more likely peril than the overdraft being called in, however, is the fluctuation of interest rates. If these go up sharply because of some economic crisis, you want to be in a position where you are keeping the facility you are using down to a minimum.

If you do need to finance the cost of purchasing a lease or essential shopfittings, however, you might sleep more easily if you have negotiated a bank loan. This would normally run for between two and five years, would have repayment periods built into it and would carry a somewhat higher rate of interest than an overdraft. Alternatively, you may need a mixed package—both overdraft facilities and a term loan.

The banks, of course, will not give you an overdraft or a loan facility automatically. The bank manager will look to see whether your application fills three criteria:

- Security—ie that his money will be safe;
- That there will be enough cash and liquid assets created to enable him to recall his money if necessary;
- That your prospects are such that you will make profitable use of the money and be able to repay capital, with interest, at agreed intervals.

The first two of these requirements are connected, but the security aspect is there simply to ensure that you use the money for the purpose for which it is intended. To cover both situations the bank will call either for liquidable assets, like shares, to be deposited with the bank as security, or for you to give a *per-*

sonal guarantee that you will repay any sums lent to you in the event that the business fails. These personal guarantees will, as we have stated earlier, override the limited liability status of a limited company and the bank will also want to ensure that you can actually meet the guarantee; for instance that you have unencumbered assets, like property, that they can take over if necessary.

If you have gone into business with others, either as a partnership or as shareholders in a limited company, there is one very important pitfall to watch out for. Normally you will agree to share the risk of a guarantee and in that case the bank will lend you the money on a 'joint and several' guarantee basis. That means, however, that if one of the parties to the agreement defaults the bank will recover the money from the other or others. For instance, if three of you borrow £10,000 'jointly and severally' and one person goes off to live on a South Sea island, the bank will look to collect £5000 each from the remaining parties if the business folds. It will be up to you, not to them, to take action against a defaulting guarantor—which reinforces the point that it is vital to know your future partners/fellow shareholders really well before you set up in business with them.

When it comes to meeting the criteria of creating sufficient assets through your business and using the bank's money profitably, things get more complicated and at this stage you will almost certainly need help from your accountant to prepare your case. The bank manager, you should note, will not normally know much about the antiques trade. He will judge your application on general business principles, looking at two key factors: profitability and cash flow.

Profitability

For the first of these factors he or she will expect to see a projection of how the business will look at the end of the first year of trading: that is to say, a picture of sales less purchases and less any stock you have left over at the end of the period. That gives a figure for gross profit. To arrive at the net profit, which is the really significant figure, you have to deduct all the other costs you will incur.

Having said that the bank manager knows nothing of antiques, he will want you to substantiate your expectations of sales and profit margins to some extent. He will want to know, for instance, how much experience you have got in the business—or in business in general, if it comes to that—where your premises will be, whether it is a neighbourhood that can reasonably be expected to provide enough customers, whether you have had loans or HP commitments before and how successful you were in meeting them, and so forth; some banks, the Natwest, for instance, actually produce a checklist of the sort of things the manager will want to know.

Trading and Profit and Loss Account for year ended 31.12.86

	£	£
Sales		40,000
Purchases	24,000	
Opening stock	4,000	
	28,000	
Less Closing stock	6,000	22,000
Gross profit		18,000
Rent and rates	2,000	
Salaries	5,500	
Heat, light	400	
Telephone	240	
Travel	600	
Repairs	400	
Depreciation	1,300	
Professional advice	300	
		10,740
Net profit		7,260

Cash flow

The other part of the story the bank manager will want to know are your cash flow projections. In terms of calculating your cash requirements these projections are even more important than the profitability at the end of the year.

The term 'cash flow projection' sounds formidably technical, but actually the sums involved are not above primary arithmetic level. All it means is that you have to work out, on a month-by-month basis for the first 12 to 18 months of your venture, how much money you have coming in and what the expenditures in each month will be. Some of the items will be absolutely predictable—rent and rates, for instance—others will be subject to intelligent guesswork. That is true of income in particular and it pays to be pessimistic. Expenditure, too, is usually higher than you expect it to be. At the end of this exercise you will find that some months produce a shortfall and it is these that the bank manager wants to know about because that is where you will need funding. He will also want to see when you will be in surplus, because this is where he would be expecting some of his money back if you are borrowing on overdraft. In assessing the situation on a loan—a fixed sum borrowed over a period of time—he would be looking for a trend where an increasing number of months would show a surplus.

It is easy to overlook items in compiling a cash flow forecast. Here are some that are common to most types of business:

- Rent
- Rates
- Telephone
- Postage
- VAT
- Heating and lighting
- Salaries
- Maintenance, repairs, cleaning
- Insurance
- Petrol, travel and subsistence
- Stationery
- Wages, PAYE, National Insurance
- Legal and accountancy fees
- Interest/loan/HP charges
- Tax

Private loans and using your own money

Even if you think that you will not need finance from the banks, either because you have enough money of your own or because you have relatives or friends willing to lend it to you, you should still get advice on cash flows and profitability. You may find, in doing your cash flows, that you will need more finance than you at first thought. As far as profitability is concerned, the question you have to ask yourself is whether your venture into the antique trade will yield more money than putting your capital into some safe investment that, at the moment, will yield about 10 per cent.

Outside lenders may also want similar reassurance. Private loans, in fact, are as rich a source of misunderstandings as partnerships, so you should be clear about all the implications of such an arrangement. The best plan is to get a solicitor to draw up the terms of the loan, covering the rate of interest, the period over which the loan is repayable and the circumstances under which it can be withdrawn. It must also be made clear to what extent, if any, the lender has any say in the running of the business and what the nature of this control is. Normally, however, the lender should not be entitled to participation in management matters; nor does the existence of his loan entitle him to a share of the profits, no matter how strong a moral claim he thinks he might have once your business starts making real money. In the case of a limited company, you must explain to the lender that a loan is not the same thing as a shareholding, though of course the offer of a loan might be conditional on acquiring shares or the option to acquire them.

Minimising your cash requirements

Borrowing money from outside sources is always expensive and, unfortunately, you will have to pay cash for most of your goods, unlike other forms of retail business where you can get 30 or even 60 days' credit. The converse is that you should make sure you yourself are paid in cash on every possible occasion.

Where you can minimise your requirements somewhat is in the purchase of other goods and materials connected with running your business. Always take the maximum amount of credit shown on the invoice; and as far as equipment is concerned, consider very carefully whether (a) you need it at all, and (b) whether leasing or HP might not be a better option than paying out a large outright sum.

Timing your VAT commitments can also be a way of minimising cash requirements. If you are planning to buy a large piece of equipment, say a van on which there is many hundreds of pounds of VAT for you to claim (assuming you are registered for VAT, of course) it will pay you to buy it at the end of your VAT quarter so that you can get your claim in as soon as possible.

Chapter 3
Professional Advice

Many people think that there is some kind of special mystique attached to membership of a profession and that any lawyer or accountant is going to do a good job for them. The fact is that while they do have useful specialist knowledge, the competence with which they apply it can be very variable. A high proportion of people who have bought a house, for instance, can tell you of errors and delays in the conveyancing process; and some accountants entrusted with their client's tax affairs have been known to send in large bills for their services, while overlooking claims for legitimate expenses that were the object of employing them in the first place.

So do not just go to the solicitor or accountant who happens to be nearest; nor should you go to someone you only know in a social capacity. Ask friends who are already in business on a similar scale, and if possible of a similar nature to your own, for recommendations. (If you already have a bank manager you know well, he may also be able to offer useful advice.) The kind of professional adviser you should be looking for at this stage is not in a big office in a central location. He will have bigger fish to fry and after the initial interview you may well be fobbed off with an assistant. Apart from that he will be expensive, for he has big office overheads to meet. On the other hand, a one-man operation can create a problem if the one man is ill or on holiday. The ideal office will be a suburban one, preferably close to where you intend to set up business because knowledge of local conditions and personalities can be invaluable, with two or three partners. Apart from that, personal impressions do count. You will probably not want to take on an adviser who immediately exudes gloomy caution, or one who appears to be a wide boy, or somebody with whom you have no rapport. Some people recommend that you should make a short list of two or three possibles and go and talk to them before making your choice.

What questions do you ask?

Later on you will be approaching your adviser about specific problems, but at the outset you and he will be exploring potential help he can give you. Begin by telling him or her something of your business plan; what sort of antiques you intend to trade in—for instance, high price, high quality items which might turn over rather slowly; cheaper pieces with smaller profit margins but rapid sales—or a mixture of both; whether you intend to open a shop or concentrate on fairs and markets; how much money you have available; what you think your financial needs are going to be over the first year of operation; how many people are going to be involved as partners or shareholders and what your plans are for the future. An accountant will want to know the range of your experience in handling accounting problems, how much help you are going to need in writing up the books and he will advise you on the basic records you should set up. Remember to ask his advice on your year end/year start; this does not have to be April 5 to April 6, and there may be sound tax reasons for choosing other dates. He may even be able to recommend the services of a part-time book-keeper to handle the mechanics, though this does not absolve you from keeping a close watch on what money is coming in and going out. It should be stressed at this point that, certainly in the case of a private limited company, the accountant you are talking to should be qualified, either through membership of the Institute of Chartered Accountants or of the Association of Certified and Corporate Accountants. Someone who advertises his services as a book-keeper or merely as an 'accountant' is not qualified to give professional advice in the true meaning of that term, though a good unqualified man can do a very adequate job in preparing tax returns for something like a small business mainly selling antiques.

A solicitor will also want to know the kind of business you are in and your plans for the future. But he will concentrate, obviously, on legal rather than financial aspects (so do not go on about money—he is a busy man, and this is only an exploratory visit). He is interested in what structure the operation is going to have and, in the case of a partnership or limited company, whether you and your colleagues have made any tentative agreements between yourselves regarding the running of the firm and the division of profits. He will want to get some idea of what kind of property you want to buy or lease and whether any planning permissions have to be sought.

How much is he going to charge?

This is rather like asking how long is a piece of string. It depends on how often you have to consult your adviser, so it is no use asking him to quote a price at the outset, though if you are lucky enough to have a very clear idea of what you want done—say, in the case of an accountant, a monthly or weekly supervision of your books, plus the preparation and auditing of your accounts—he may give you a rough idea of what his charges will be. Alternatively, he may suggest an annual retainer for these services and any advice directly concerned with them, plus extra charges for anything that falls outside them, like a complicated wrangle with the inspector of taxes about allowable items. When calculating the likely cost of using an accountant remember that his fees are tax deductible.

An annual retainer is a less suitable way of dealing with your solicitor because your problems are likely to be less predictable than those connected with accounting and book-keeping. A lot of your queries may be raised, and settled, on the telephone: the 'Can I do this?' type. Explaining that kind of problem on the telephone is usually quicker and points can be more readily clarified than by writing a letter setting out the facts of the case (though you should ask for confirmation in writing in matters where you could be legally liable in acting on the advice you have been given!). However, asking advice on the telephone can be embarrassing for both parties. You will be wondering whether your solicitor is charging you for it and either way it could inhibit you from discussing the matter fully. You should, therefore, check at the outset what the procedure is for telephone enquiries and how these are accounted for on your bill.

A guide—not a crutch

For someone starting in business on their own, facing for the first time 'the loneliness of thought and the agony of decision', there is a temptation to lean on professional advisers too much. Apart from the fact that this can be very expensive, it is a bad way to run a business. Before you lift the telephone or write a letter, think. Is this clause in a contract something you could figure out for yourself if you sat down and concentrated on reading it carefully? Would it not be better to check through the ledger yourself to find out where to put some item of expenditure that is not immediately classifiable? Only get in touch with your advisers when you are genuinely stumped for an answer, not just because you cannot be bothered to think it out for yourself. Remember, too, that nobody can make up your mind for you on matters of policy. If you feel, for example, that you cannot work with your partner, the only thing your solicitor can or should do for you is to tell you how to dissolve the partnership, not whether it should be done at all.

Your bank manager

The other person with whom you should make contact when you start up in business is your bank manager. The importance of picking a unit of the right size which we have mentioned in connection with professional advice also holds true in this case. A smaller local branch is more likely to be helpful towards the problems of a small business than one in a central urban location with a lot of big accounts among its customers. You might also discuss, with your accountant, the possibility of going outside the 'big four'. It is necessary to be careful here because there have been some notorious failures of 'fringe banks', but there are a number of solid smaller banking houses who are more accommodating about charges on handling your account and loans. If you are changing banks, as opposed to merely switching branches, it will be difficult for you to get a sizeable overdraft until the manager has seen something of your track record.

You must inform your bank manager of your intention to set up in business, providing him with much the same information as you gave to your accountant. Indeed, it is quite a good idea to ask your accountant to come along to this first meeting, so that he can explain any technicalities.

Chapter 4
What Type of Business?

Having decided to start an antiques business and made suitable preparation in acquiring basic knowledge, you have to decide on the type of set-up that will suit you. You may be lucky in having sufficient capital to buy a property, or you may prefer to rent a shop or gallery. Some feel safer dealing from home or 'running' and others are happy to keep their overheads as low as possible by conducting all their business from a market stall.

Fairs and market stalls

Periodic fairs and charity events are held in most small towns and many villages, and they offer widely varying standards from the unashamedly junky to the posh and pricey. It is as well to do some research before embarking on a stall of your own. Go for unpretentious but well-frequented venues: smart surroundings usually cost more but will not necessarily attract more buyers. Sunday and bank holiday fairs are said to be much more successful than Saturday events. A few people even make their entire living by taking stands at one-day fairs. They will work every Saturday, Sunday and bank holiday at different fairs, and spend the remaining days of the week out buying. The weekly antiques trade papers as well as local periodicals give details of forthcoming fairs, including the organisers' telephone numbers.

Both market stalls and fairs can be lucrative, but there is always the discouraging possibility that you will travel many miles to a pitch, unpack and display all your stock (usually humped about in cardboard boxes) and then sit all day without making enough profit to cover expenses. On the other hand, one dull day in an antiques fair is probably less costly than a long slack period in a shop which carries considerable overheads, and it is probably a good idea for the novice dealer to start in a small way and move to more permanent premises once he or she has become established. A stall in a weekly antiques market can cost as little as £8 or so and may be reduced if you share with a friend. A pitch in a regularly held fair may range from about £10-£30 per day or more, depending on the venue and the prestige of the event itself.

The full-time indoor markets and emporiums such as Grays or Antiquarius in London, and similar centres in many provincial towns and cities, can also provide a comparatively inexpensive way into dealing from one's own premises. Working alongside other dealers can be an advantage and provide companionship in slack periods, although some find the lack of privacy disconcerting, especially if their neighbours turn out to be the inquisitive sort, and gloom can be catching. However, the magnetic effect of a large conglomeration of dealers on potential buyers, as well as the comparative security of an indoor market, should outweigh any disadvantages, and some antiques centres are run on a cooperative basis by which dealers take turns to look after a group of stands, enabling the owners to go out on buying trips.

Dealing from home

There is actually no need to set up a stall or shop anywhere: many dealers run successful antiques businesses from home. Freed from the constraints of shop opening hours, as well as the extra overheads of a showroom, they prefer to spend the maximum time out buying. Some take stands at fairs from time to time, while others rely entirely on telephoned appointments from potential customers. This system certainly cuts out time-wasting browsers and ensures that only serious buyers are likely to come round. A dealer from home will gradually build up contacts with fellow dealers who may make regular calls to his house. Many dealers from home sell only to the trade, but some advertise in their local newspapers, in antiques magazines or directories, and welcome non-trade visitors as well.

Running

Dealing from home can be combined with 'running', that is, taking goods to other dealers to sell. A runner is an itinerant dealer who goes out and finds markets instead of waiting for buyers to come to him. In effect, he generally does his selling from the back of a car or van. To be successful, a runner needs a good deal of skill in judging other dealers' tastes as well as the knowledge to buy the right goods. While few runners admit that they buy specifically for other dealers, they may have certain individuals in mind as potential buyers when they make purchases. If a runner is to sell to a dealer on a regular basis he has to be fairly accurate in gauging what will appeal to him. In other words, a runner needs to know as much about buyers as about buying.

Part of the appeal of running is the ability to 'make things happen' by going out and finding buyers; a runner probably has more control over both buying and selling his goods than any other kind of dealer. It is hard work and a runner must be constantly alive to opportunities and almost permanently on the road, but it can be a lucrative and stimulating life for the committed.

Knockers

Mention must be made here of the disreputable practice of 'knocking', or what is more politely known as making 'uninvited calls upon private domestic premises'. A considerable number of heartless rogues within the antiques trade make a practice of knocking on the doors of people's houses and asking if they have antiques to sell. For every two or three people who tell the knocker fairly and squarely to go away, there is likely to be one (often a naive and impecunious old lady) who unwisely allows him inside her house and falls for his compliments about the old furniture or the pretty ornaments on the mantelpiece. The chances are that the knocker will make an offer for several items which will be well below the market value but may nevertheless impress the victim, unaware of modern prices, and he will make off with considerable bargains. The practice of knocking is regarded as totally unethical by the antiques trade establishment, and is a form of imposition which falls little short of theft.

Opening a shop

If you decide to take on a shop you must obviously begin by working out the finances involved. If you have a capital sum available for the whole venture and intend to buy a property outright, you must ensure that you still have enough money left to buy stock, pay yourself a basic wage and take care of running costs and contingencies which may arise. Similarly, if you plan to rent your premises you must work out how much rent you can afford after allowing for the needs of stock and personal survival.

Chapter 5

Premises

The actual position of your shop or gallery can be crucial, but it is often difficult to determine what is a good site. Most people agree that it is an advantage to be in a street or area where there are other antique shops, particularly with regard to trade buyers, who will feel it worth their while to visit a locality where there are plenty of calls to make and the possibility of fruitful hunting. A dealer is unlikely to travel a long way off his route to visit a solitary antique shop unless it is known to be a reliable supplier of the types of goods he wants, whereas he may call at any shops he finds on his way round a particular patch. Dealers working in the same street or village can sometimes help each other by directing visitors to neighbouring shops whenever it seems appropriate.

Shops on busy roads can be at a disadvantage unless there is plenty of parking space nearby, and some town-based dealers have suffered greatly from fast-flowing one-way systems and clearways being routed past their premises, making it difficult for would-be callers to stop. On the other hand, residential districts and quiet back streets can be lifeless simply because they are never noticed by passers-by.

Size of premises

The size of your premises will to a large extent be determined by the money you have available and the kind of stock in which you intend to trade. Furniture obviously takes up more room than ceramics or jewellery, but it is surprising how much one can fit into a fairly small space, and it is probably more economic to have smaller premises enticingly crammed with stock than a large showroom with the goods scattered sparsely about, giving an impression of shortage of stock.

When choosing your shop try to find one with storage space at the back or in an outbuilding; you will be surprised how useful it is. A back room where you can not only make a cup of coffee but also undertake minor repairs and renovations is almost essential. You will certainly need to keep packaging materials such as cardboard boxes and old newspapers, as well as more elegant tissue paper and other wrappings, and these take up a good deal of room.

An antique shop incorporating living accommodation can be a distinct advantage, not only from the point of view of security, but also because it allows more flexibility. It may enable you to run the shop without extra help, and out-of-hours calls can be more easily covered. Overheads like rates and fuel bills may be reduced, as well as the cost of travelling to and from work.

Shipping goods
The largest premises are generally required by dealers in 'shipping goods'. Whole warehouses piled up with second-hand furniture which may or may not be technically antique began to proliferate some years ago in response to a lively demand from abroad for highly commercial and often good quality furnishings. They are sent by the container-load to America (North and South), Australia, New Zealand, South Africa, the Middle East and Europe, to be sold in the 'antique' shops or at auction in those countries. While different kinds of goods are especially favoured in different countries, age has little to do with demand; condition is more important, and reproduction items of the right sort can find ready markets.

Although the shipping business is no longer booming it can still be lucrative for those who have a good eye for the 'commercial lot' and the energy to gather together vast quantities of mediocre items. It is not for the fastidious or those who feel sentimental about exporting Britain's heritage, however mundane. The dealer in shipping goods is generally a shrewd businessman who regards antiques merely as commodities, saleable by the container-load.

Clients

At this point it is probably a good idea to focus on the types of clients you are likely to have. While certain forms of antique dealing, notably being a runner and dealing in shipping goods, involve working almost exclusively within 'the trade', practically every dealer must rely heavily on trade sales as well as retail. Those with the highest proportion of private buyers are likely to be the exclusive entrepreneurs of Bond Street, St James's and Belgravia, whose goods are generally too expensive to allow another dealer's profit except in rare circumstances. Others, mostly specialists, make a point of cultivating collectors and over the years may build up a preponderance of retail customers. For the rest, the trade is likely to constitute at least 50 per cent of business, and in many cases more. Indeed some dealers prefer to sell only to the trade and may put up signs like 'Trade buyers welcome' or 'Trade only please'.

How many customers from overseas you will attract depends largely on where your premises are situated. Obviously, London dealers are likely to have the highest proportion of foreign clients, but those in areas around ports serving continental routes—Sussex, Kent and parts of East Anglia are among them—will attract trade dealers on buying trips from Europe. Whether you choose to stock the kinds of goods that suit foreign tastes will clearly determine whether or not they become regular customers.

Arrangement

How you arrange your stock in your shop, gallery or warehouse is of course a matter of choice and taste as well as conscious policy. Some people like everything neatly and artistically arranged, with the furniture polished and the surfaces free of dust. These people will affirm that the window display is of paramount importance and should be changed regularly. Others like a cluttered effect, with every available space filled, to give a bargain basement illusion. Of course, the idea that you pay more for the goods in the carefully arranged shop and less in the dusty cluttered atmosphere of the crowded one is completely erroneous, but there may be a psychological effect, at least on retail buyers. However you arrange your goods, it is advisable to label them clearly (see page 82). A dealer should have the confidence to proclaim his prices and to describe his goods properly.

Breakages

With a crowded shop you may run a higher risk of breakages, and in this respect carelessly carried handbags are probably the worst culprits. Some dealers display the rather forbidding sign 'All breakages must be paid for', and obviously most people would expect to reimburse a dealer for any damage they have knowingly caused, but there may be difficulties, such as the case where the visitor insists that the item was placed so precariously that it dropped almost before it was touched, or that it was a repaired piece which 'just fell apart in my hands'. Problems may arise if the broken item had no price label attached—another good reason for labelling your stock. In fact, 'all breakages must be paid for' has practically no force in law, and the dealer has to rely on the courtesy and consideration of his clients in this matter, or make certain that he is covered by insurance for these eventualities (see page 53).

Security

Security is a perennial problem for the antique dealer. There have been so many serious crimes in which shop owners and their assistants have been held at gunpoint or tied up while their premises have been ransacked, that many dealers now keep their doors permanently locked. Visitors have to ring the bell and the dealer at least has the opportunity to see them before they are admitted. This system is likely to deter criminal gangs, and it certainly gives dealers and their assistants a greater feeling of personal safety.

Dealers in jewellery and silver are particularly at risk, and many can recount horrifying experiences of being followed and eventually mugged after fruitful buying trips. Women, who tend to carry small valuables in their handbags, are especially vulnerable.

Within the shop it is important to keep pocket-sized trinkets in display cases or cupboards which can be opened on request. Do not be tempted to improve your display by leaving small items scattered about on the furniture. Running an antiques shop is like playing Kim's game. You have to be constantly awake to the possibility of theft, and be able to notice quickly if anything goes missing. The frequency with which goods are 'lifted' from antique shops and stalls is a distressing fact of life, but speedy reactions can at least alert the neighbours to the presence of a thief in the locality, and may lead to his apprehension.

Arranging the shop in such a way as to deter the light-fingered is not always easy: many thieves work in pairs, and while one keeps you occupied in conversation about an item, the other is free to pocket the odd treasure. A favourite device of the solitary thief is to ask the price of an item at the back of the shop, or behind something else, and while you are looking, with your back turned, he can help himself to something small. Without being unfriendly, it is as well to be somewhat suspicious of strange visitors, however charming or apparently knowledgeable.

Burglar alarms
Many insurance companies insist that dealers install burglar alarms in their premises before they will cover them and, in any case, most dealers regard an intruder alarm as an essential precaution. Several types of system are available, and often they are installed in combination. The most usual are a scanner to detect the movement of bodies in a given area, electrical contacts on doors and windows, and pressure mats on the floor. The signalling system nearly always consists of a bell or siren which rings outside the premises and, preferably, inside as well.

A strobe light can be attached to this—an advantage in remote areas, and a great help to patrolling policemen.

Some burglar alarms also operate through the telephone system, to alert the police with a 999 call and a pre-recorded message, or to contact the central station of the burglar alarm company through a digital communicator. This gives a print-out and conveys more details of the emergency than the 999 type of call direct to the police. For example, it can specifically record the pressing of the 'personal attack' button, which should bring the police to the premises at a rather hotter pace than a mere message recording that the burglar alarm is ringing.

The British Standards Institute in British Standard 4737 lays down standards to which all intruder alarms must conform, both as regards equipment and the way it is installed and maintained. There is also a watchdog body, the National Supervisory Council for Intruder Alarms, set up by the burglar alarm industry in collaboration with insurance companies, to examine alarms installed by its members and to make sure they conform to high standards. An insurance company should accept an alarm installed by any member company of the NSCIA, even though in practice insurance agents sometimes try to promote specific burglar alarm companies. Often these are perfectly reputable, but it is a good idea to seek comparative estimates from other companies before having an alarm system installed.

Fire protection

Fire is one of the risks for which every antique dealer should be prepared. As well as commonsense precautions like using safe forms of heating rather than paraffin stoves or open electric fires and so on, make sure you have an adequate number of fire extinguishers on your premises. Electric wiring should be regularly checked, especially around spotlights which can easily overheat, and smokers should be discouraged. A fire alarm device or heat detector may be appropriate, in which case you should seek advice from the

Fire Protection Association. The legal requirements for fire protection are set out in the *Guide to Fire Precautions 1971 Act No 3: Offices, Shops and Railway Premises*, and this is available from HMSO.

Chapter 6
Insurance

There is no sphere of the antiques trade in which professional advice is more important than in that of insurance. The hazards are almost endless and it would be an unusual business that did not encounter some of them at one point. Margaret Browne, who organises some of the major fairs in the London area, says it is almost inevitable that there will be at least one case of theft or breakage on every occasion. It is very hard to get redress in the latter instance and equally hard to detect the former. There are, in fact, known thieves and kleptomaniacs around and one of the advantages of selling at fairs, she says, is that they can be refused admission at the door because they are generally known to the organisers even if they have never actually been caught red-handed. She cites the case of two little old ladies whose appearance at any fair always coincided with the disappearance of jewellery on a widespread scale.

As for breakages, she says that though a customer causing them is theoretically liable for negligence, this is virtually impossible to prove in law unless a customer actually picked up a piece and dropped it in the presence of witnesses. Otherwise the customer could claim that the piece had been badly balanced on the display or that he or she had been jostled while handling it.

Theft and damage at fairs are, however, only two of the many risks which a dealer has to face. Items can be broken in a shop, or in transit, or at a restorers. It can even happen at the auctioneers, and once the hammer has fallen the winning bidder is responsible for its safety. And it is not only members of the public who can be the cause of breakage or damage. It can happen to you or to your employees or be caused by pets.

As for theft, that comes in many shapes and sizes, ranging from 'lifting' small items of jewellery to wholesale break-ins. In the latter case, the loss of stock is often accompanied by damage to the premises such as broken showcases, windows, or security equipment. Whatever cash is around is usually taken as well. Furthermore, the damage to your premises resulting from a violent break-in may be such that you will not be able to open until you can get repairs done. Stock losses may also take time to make good. The indirect loss of trade can be very serious but it is possible to insure against it by taking out additional cover against 'consequential loss'. Insurers are not keen to cover this as a routine risk because of the prolonged period and general uncertainty of replacing stock in an antique shop.

Another indirect hazard is that of accidentally purchasing stolen goods. To do so knowingly is, of course, a criminal offence, but even if you bought them in the belief that they were honestly acquired, if it does turn out that they were stolen you will have to return them to their rightful owner without recompense. In the case of a valuable item quite large amounts of money can be involved. It is, however, also possible—and highly advisable in view of the quantity of stolen goods now circulating—to insure against what is called 'defective title'. In fact all the risks referred to can and should be covered by insurance. This extends even to breakages caused by the negligence of customers, though if it was provable the insurers would try to mitigate their loss by taking action against the person responsible.

There is, however, one area of customer relationships which cannot be covered by insurance in the normal course of events. If a customer leaves a piece with you for safe-keeping, or if you hang on to it without purchasing it for any reason—perhaps to get a further opinion on its value—it remains the customer's liability from an insurance point of view. This should be pointed out to them and may act as an inducement to them not to use your shop as a temporary warehouse, as some trade customers are apt to do.

Another risk area which is not covered by insurance

is if you accept a stolen or dud cheque. The advice given by those with experience in the trade is never to part with goods against cheques from strangers without first clearing them through the bank; and indeed to accept them only from customers of proven reliability and integrity. Where they are backed by bankers' cards you do, of course, have cover from the bank in question—but only up to the limit of the card which is stated on the back. (If you are on the Joint Credit Cards Scheme, incidentally, remember the limit they have given you for the value you can accept. If the transaction runs over that you will have to obtain clearance with the company that has issued the card.)

Choosing a broker

Insurance is generally taken out through an insurance broker but the vast majority of brokers are unfamiliar with the problems of the antique trade. The *Insurance Buyer's Guide*, published by Kluwer does give details of some brokers with special knowledge in this field, but a firm which indubitably has it is Sneath, Kent & Stuart Ltd (172 Bishopsgate, London EC2M 4NQ, Tel 01-283 8306). They are recommended by LAPADA, to whose members they give a 20 per cent discount on premiums and Geoffrey Sneath, who is himself married to an antique dealer, has an unusual amount of first-hand knowledge of the trade. Stewart Wrightson Ltd of 1 Camomile Street, London EC3 and Thomas R Miller & Son (Insurance) Ltd of 14 St Mary Axe, London EC3, have also both offered special antique dealer policies for many years.

There are quite a number of variables in the type of risk involved which affect the amount of the premium you will be quoted, so in the first instance you will have to fill in a detailed proposal form which gives the broker some idea of the kind of business you are engaged in, and the premises from which you are conducting it. Particularly he will want to know:

● The age and state of the premises

- Whether or not they are permanently occupied
- Whether you do any other work there, such as restoration
- Where the stock is kept
- What its maximum value is at any time, broken down by categories
- What security precautions are in force
- What maximum values you have in transit at any time
- To what extent you exhibit at fairs, markets and open-air stalls and what values are represented (only limited cover may be available in the latter type of trading)
- Details of the window display area and to what extent that is protected.

If the values to be insured are over £10,000, the brokers will send along a surveyor to look at the security arrangements, make stipulations about how they should be improved and check the stock valuations in the proposal. The point of this latter move is that insurers do not 'average out' claims as is the case with ordinary domestic insurance. There, if you are insured for, say £50,000, and the true value of what you are covering turns out to be £100,000, you receive only 50 per cent of the loss.

Other types of cover

There are, of course, several other kinds of cover you will have to obtain when you set up a business, but it helps if they are all organised by one broker—though incidentally, if you already have a broker who is not at home with the antiques business, he can arrange the special cover you need through a specialist company. Risks that are common to all businesses and which you have to provide for are:

- Insurance of the building
- Motor insurance
- Employer's liability, if you employ staff
- Public liability in case you cause injury to a member of the public or their premises in the course of business. You will also need third

party public liability if you employ staff or
work with partners
- Insurance against losing your driving licence.

There may also be other risks which your broker will
suggest you should cover and which depend somewhat on personal circumstances, for instance whether
you should take out a policy to cover the situation if
you fall ill and someone else has to manage the business in your absence.

Insurance is relatively inexpensive. In London, for
example, the average premium for ordinary domestic
'contents' insurance is now 1 per cent; Sneath, Kent
& Stuart charge 0.6 per cent in the same region on
furniture and from 1.25 per cent for smaller, more
high-risk items. As in the case of domestic insurance,
there are no 'no claims' bonuses.

Insurance premiums are, of course, fully allowable
against tax inasmuch as they are incurred wholly in
respect of your business. A typical example of the
business risks you ought to cover in relation to an
antiques business is given in the prospectus repro-
duced below (courtesy Sneath, Kent & Stuart).

THE COVER AVAILABLE

I Contents
Consisting of stock, fixtures, fittings, showcases, equipment, reference books, decorations and improvements, grilles, shop blinds.

Cover: For shops or persons trading from home
All risks of physical loss or damage whilst at the proposers business premises, at fairs or on exhibition, at repairers and restorers
premises, at private and/or commercial clients premises, at auction rooms and at own house. Transit risks anywhere in the United
Kingdom are also included as are postal sendings anywhere in the
world.

*Cover: For persons trading from antiques centres
and the like*
Insurance cover can be arranged as mentioned in I above if the
protections for stock (eg showcases are locked other than when
they are being worked) are adequate, otherwise the cover is limited to:

All Risks of Physical Loss or Damage but excluding theft from the
Assured's Premises or portion of the premises occupied by the

Assured, unless following forcible and/or violent entry or exit thereto or therefrom but including smash and grab and/or hold-up. The cover is all risks of physical loss or damage whilst stock is at fairs or on exhibition, at repairers' and restorers' premises, at private and/or commercial clients' premises, at auction rooms and at your own house.

Transit risks anywhere in the United Kingdom are also included as are postal sendings anywhere in the world.

II Consequential Loss

Loss of Gross Profit following loss or damage at the business premises of the proposer by any perils other than Burglary and theft, or any attempt thereat, smash and grab and hold-up or damage done by thieves.

III Money

Comprising cash, cheques, postal and money orders, and securities for money.

Cover: on money whilst in transit to and from the bank, at business premises in and out of normal working hours (subject to protections) and whilst in transit elsewhere in the United Kingdom or at the private residence of the proposer. The standard limits for the latter extension is £500 any one loss. However these may be amended upon application.

IV (a) Legal Liability to the Public

Provides indemnity for accidental personal injury and accidental damage to property of the public including food and drink supplied and delivery risks.
Limit of Indemnity £500,000 any one occurrence.

IV (b) Products Liability

Limit of Indemnity £500,000 in the year.

V Legal Liability to Employees

Provides unlimited legal liability for accidents to employees arising in the course of their employment.

VI (a) Bodily Injury Assault

Cover: On principals or employees for benefits of death or disablement caused by injury sustained as a result of Robbery, hold-up or any attempt thereat.

Minimum suggested benefit £5,000 Death/Loss of eyes or limbs or permanent disablement and £50 weekly benefit during temporary total disablement.
Premium £2.50 per annum per person.

VI (b) Personal Accident

Cover: On principals or employees for benefits of death or disablement caused by injury sustained from any accidental cause occurring at any time during 24 hours of the day.

VII Defective Title

Indemnity for loss resulting from goods purchased during the course of normal trading to which the proposer subsequently finds that they have no legal title.

VIII Fidelity

Cover for money, securities and stock against misappropriation by employees.

IX Buildings

Cover: All risks of physical Loss or Damage subject to normal excesses.

X Glass in Shop Front, External Showcases, External Signs

Cover: All risks of physical loss or damage.

XI Householders Comprehensive Insurance and Personal All Risks Insurance

Many other additional covers are also available.

Please answer the appropriate questions:

1. ANTIQUE AND FINE ART DEALERS

   (a) **Type of Stock.** *Delete items not applicable:*
      Jewellery, Silver, Silver Plate, Furniture, Clocks,
      Watches, China, Glass, Porcelain, Pictures, Paintings,
      Bronzes, Pewter, Brass Copper, Dolls, Objets d'Art.
   (b) Estimated value of Stock (at Cost Price) £ . . . .
      Renewal date of existing policy . . . .

2. BUILDING INSURANCE FOR BUSINESS PREMISES £. . . . .

Renewal date of existing policy . . . .

3. MOTOR INSURANCE

Number of Commercial Vehicles . . . .
Renewal date of existing policy . . . .
Number of Private Cars . . . .
Renewal date of existing policy . . . .

4. COMPREHENSIVE INSURANCE ON BUILDINGS AND CONTENTS OF PRIVATE DWELLINGS AND/OR PERSONAL ALL RISKS COVER

Renewal date of existing policy . . . .

5. LIFE ASSURANCE

6. SELF-EMPLOYED PENSION SCHEME WITH FULL TAX RELIEF

7. PERMANENT HEALTH INSURANCE
We require to know your age next birthday for
Nos 5 to 7 . . . .

8. HOUSE PURCHASE

9. BOAT INSURANCE
Renewal of existing policy . . . .

Chapter 7
Buying

Buying is the most important aspect of dealing in antiques, ranking above selling and practically all other aspects of trade. It is often said, 'If you have the right goods they'll sell themselves'. Dealers are constantly asked where they find things, and few can or will answer the question. The reason is usually that they find stock in all kinds of places and do not have many regular sources of supply: even if they did, they would not divulge them. Unlike a grocery or other commodity business, there are no fixed ways of acquiring goods, and while there are generally accepted methods of search, there are no financial or geographical limits. Tedious and sometimes fruitless journeys there may be, but occasional surprises and excitements will reward the persevering.

Buying antiques has in many ways become much more difficult recently: the supply of genuine good pieces is obviously dwindling, and prices are consequently rising; people in general are now much more knowledgeable and many more are collecting and/or dealing, so there are enormous numbers of people searching for fewer and fewer goods. Faking has become a fine art. However, it is still perfectly possible to find real bargains, and many people do; even if one excludes the occasional streak of luck there are constant opportunities to buy items at prices which allow a profit on resale. But you must be prepared to search hard and often.

Out on the road

While no possible source—from West End gallery to local jumble sale—should be dismissed, in practice most professional dealers follow certain patterns in

61

their buying. Having discovered the most fruitful places for them (and everyone has different tastes and requirements, so what suits one dealer may not suit another) they tend to make regular trips in these directions. This may involve driving over a set route through certain parts of the country, making calls to dealers' shops and possibly taking in an auction sale on the way. Sometimes a tour of London dealers will be undertaken, and while it is obviously not possible to visit every shop and gallery, each dealer soon discovers which are most in tune with his own tastes and which are likely to have suitable goods at the right prices.

While a set route for buying may save time and petrol, most dealers like to make occasional forays into new territory both for the sake of interest and the possibility of discovering fresh pastures. Many dealers who may cover huge mileages in search of stock in far distant parts of the country will fight shy of combing the shops in their own locality, because they feel that locally bought goods will not be 'fresh'.

A high proportion of dealers, with some justification, maintain that London is the cheapest place for antiques. Their conclusion is based not only on prices but on the huge breadth of choice in a comparatively small area. It is not for nothing that London is the acknowledged centre of the world's art and antiques market. People are often astonished at the high price tags on antiques in the country, since many assume that goods are bound to be cheaper out of London. This is obviously a fallacy, and it is impossible to generalise: there are 'expensive' and 'cheap' dealers both in and out of London; their pricing depends on the profit margins they require as well as on the amount they pay for individual items, apart from considerations like overheads, mileages involved in finding stock and, the most variable factor of all, what they feel they can demand. Where competition is toughest, that is, in London, prices may well be most competitive.

While a good many dealers divide their buying trips between London and set routes in the country according to a fairly regular pattern, some have a much less systematic approach. They may enjoy exploring 'virgin' territory even if it means many wasted miles of driving, and prefer to try different areas on practically every trip. Some use the salerooms more than others, and well-publicised country auctions can attract dealers from long distances: they are then likely to tour the vicinity scanning the shops as well. Even during their holidays, few dealers can resist poking about in the local antique shops, however unpromising they may seem.

Buying at auction

For sheer entertainment there is little to beat an auction, whether it be one of those grand occasions when the apparently irresistible contents of a stately home are sold for breath-taking sums or whether it is simply a sale of 'chattels' cleared from a few houses in a small-town district. For both appeal to our gambling instincts, and both can generate feelings of excitement and suspense which have a strong attraction even for the most level-headed. Besides, there is always the chance, if not the likelihood, of a bargain.

There are antique dealers who very rarely buy at auction: they dislike the public nature of the event and find the processes of pre-sale viewing somewhat tedious, especially if it is outside their immediate neighbourhood. Others, however, enjoy the camaraderie of the saleroom and find the auction a fruitful source of stock: these will travel long distances to attend sales, and never miss an opportunity to buy in their local rooms. In a curious way they may feel more confident buying in public competition than in a dealer's showroom. The majority of dealers probably fall between these two extremes, using the saleroom as well as other sources for providing stock.

One major advantage of the saleroom as far as the dealer is concerned is the fact that it releases a high proportion of privately owned goods on to the market. Many people use auctions as a means of disposing of antiques and household furnishings they know little about but from which they hope to make as much capital as possible. While they often find it tricky to sell directly to a dealer, they have more confidence in the auction system as a means of raising a fair price. In some cases they are certainly justified. Because so much antique trading is done between dealers, such 'private' sources of stock are eagerly sought, and it is often surprising how high auction prices will go for items of known private provenance. Indeed, it has become widely accepted that prices at a large country house sale can vastly exceed those to be expected even in the major London auction houses. Because of this it is not unknown for goods to be sent from London to one of these country house sales in the hope that they will attract higher bids. In these cases, mention should be made in the catalogue of 'other property' or some similar indication that certain goods have come from a different source.

Obviously, the prices reached at an auction will depend largely on who is there, and a well-publicised sale may attract too many serious buyers to leave many bargains. On the other hand, there can be specialist items which attract few people, or rarities which hardly anybody recognises. It is surprising how few people, even 'professionals', viewing a sale are totally thorough: they may take the catalogue as gospel (which it rarely can be, so speedily are most compiled) and fail to look beyond the printed description at the object itself; or they may simply not notice the one good item in a job lot. Pictures, particularly portfolios of drawings or prints, are often cursorily glanced at and passed over by sale viewers, while a careful inspection can reveal something of high quality or rarity which may well have escaped the attention of the hard-pressed cataloguer.

Using catalogue information

When viewing a sale it pays to read the catalogue descriptions and then study carefully the goods themselves. Furniture should be turned upside down and examined all over for evidence of alteration or restoration, and ceramics, glass, textiles, jewellery and metalwork scrutinised for repairs and damage as well as basic quality. Pictures also require painstaking examination. No time spent looking will be wasted, and much can be learned.

While cataloguers often have to work under considerable pressure and no saleroom expert should be regarded as infallible—or would claim to be—sale catalogues can be an invaluable tool for buyers. Where specialised sales in the major auction houses are concerned, the catalogues can constitute important guides to a subject, the results of considerable scholarship and careful research. The importance of good catalogues in publicising sales cannot be overestimated, and has been exploited increasingly in recent years.

In the small provincial auction rooms, catalogues may be prepared by 'generalists', that is, experts who are not specialists in a particular field like furniture or pictures, but whose nets range widely over the whole field of antiques. While they may have enormous experience and wide knowledge, they obviously cannot have an equal grasp of every aspect of antiques and their catalogues are likely to be useful basic guides to the lots in the sale rather than scholarly appraisals. Full use should be made of them, but at the same time a dealer should have the confidence to make his own judgement of the items in question, even if his opinion differs from that of the cataloguer.

Before embarking on a buying spree in an auction room read the notices and conditions of sale which are generally printed at the beginning of the catalogue and note whether there is a buyer's premium or not. Many salerooms inflict a charge of 10 per cent of the hammer price (plus VAT) on buyers, and this must obviously be a consideration in bidding. Take in the rules about paying for and collecting the lots you buy: failure to comply with them can cost you money as well as inconvenience. Knowing your responsibilities regarding your purchases is also important: some auctioneers maintain that the buyer's responsibility begins when the hammer goes down while others give a few days' grace. If the item is lost or damaged after you have bought it you may not be compensated.

If, on the other hand, items are lost or damaged

before they are sold, buyers, even commission bidders, are not responsible. In the case of a commission buyer discovering that the lot he bid for has been broken or part of it has gone missing between the time he viewed it and the time he came to collect his purchase, he should be able to expect some redress from the auctioneer, who can either cancel the sale or negotiate a reduced price. If a breakage is discovered before the sale begins, it is obviously the auctioneer's duty not to execute commission bids for the lot in question.

It is as well to acquaint yourself with the nuances of catalogue jargon. With regard to furniture, an item described as 'Sheraton period' should belong to the late eighteenth or early nineteenth centuries, whereas a 'Sheraton style' piece is likely to be a later reproduction. Some auctioneers helpfully obviate the confusion this habit of phraseology can cause by selling 'Victorian dining chairs in the Chippendale style' or 'a nineteenth-century Queen Anne chest' and so on, leaving the viewer in no doubt as to the approximate age of the objects in question.

Pictures come in for quite precise description. One recorded in the catalogue as being by Joseph Bloggs is, in the auctioneer's opinion, definitely by him; where an artist's first name is unknown, a series of asterisks followed by the surname indicates the same opinion. A picture by 'J. Bloggs' is of his period and may have been treated to a few of his own brush strokes, while one labelled simply 'Bloggs' is likely to be merely in his style or painted by one of his followers. Similarly, the expression 'signed' and/or 'dated' means the auctioneer reckons that the signature is genuinely that of the artist it purports to be, and the date inscribed by him, while 'bears signature' and/or 'date' means he thinks it is likely that the inscription has been added by another hand.

Terms like 'attributed to', 'ascribed to', 'circle of', 'follower of', 'manner of', 'school', 'after', and so on, are used to indicate fine differences of the auctioneer's opinion regarding the authenticity or period of a picture, and may vary slightly from one auction house to another. The explanation of terms at the front or back of the catalogue should make these shades of meaning clear.

Bidding

Having decided that you want to acquire an item to be auctioned you should assess what it is worth to you. Your price estimate should include the buyer's premium if any, and allow for possible restoration costs, re-upholstering, reframing and so on, as well as your profit when you resell. Once you have fixed on a price it is advisable to stick to it and not be tempted to go on bidding when it has been overtaken. This can be extremely difficult, and to avoid being carried away some people make it their habit to leave bids with the auctioneer. This also avoids the necessity of attending the actual sale as well as the viewing.

When filling in your bidding slip, check the lot number carefully and write a description of the piece with it, checking that the item you have seen is in the right sale. It is customary in some auction houses for uncollected items from previous sales to be left in the room, and it is all too easy to bid unwittingly for a piece that has been sold already. As well as a lot number, every item should be marked with a date. When you leave your slip with the clerk, it is a good idea to check the lot numbers and descriptions with him to avoid any mistakes.

The system of leaving bids with an auctioneer has sometimes come under criticism: it seems that not every saleroom is scrupulous in observing the principle that commission bids 'are to be executed as cheaply as is permitted by other bids, or reserves, if any'. Obviously, it is tempting for an auctioneer, when faced with a commission bid on his books of £200, and a sea of blank faces and no bids beyond £150 in the room, to knock the piece down (or up) to the commission bidder for £190 rather than £155 or £160. The buyer has no way of knowing whether there was in fact an underbidder on the auctioneer's books or not, so there is virtually no redress. A commission buyer's suspicions may be justifiably aroused if he or she habitually finds that lots at a certain saleroom are secured for the commission bid price or one very close to it. Sometimes those present at an auction may notice that an uncharacteristically high number of items are knocked down for much higher prices than the bids in the room might suggest, and it may not be unjust to conclude that the auctioneer is using his initiative a little too actively in the interests of the vendor and, of course, himself.

It should be said most emphatically that these imputations of malpractice may be laid at the door of comparatively few auctioneers: most act in a perfectly proper way, and find no difficulty in reconciling their role as agents of the vendor with the free and fair progress of the auction system.

But for these and other reasons, many dealers do not make a habit of leaving commission bids with the auctioneer or his clerk. If they cannot be present at a sale they prefer to leave their bids with a porter. He will write them, preferably in code, into his catalogue and then bid personally at the sale, without recourse to the auctioneer's book. If he secures an item for an individual for a low price he can expect to receive a correspondingly generous tip. Obviously, dealers who regularly visit particular auction rooms will get to know individual porters, and it can be a great advantage for a dealer to cultivate such professional friendships. While porters should be too discreet to quote reserves, they often know the sorts of prices likely to secure a lot, and may give useful hints to the trusted few.

Do not leave a bid before a sale and then come to it and bid in person: perhaps such a mistake seems too obvious to need pointing out, but it has been known for an over-enthusiastic buyer to bid against himself and more than double up the price of an item without realising that the underbidder was a saleroom employee acting on his own behalf!

Most salerooms will accept a telephoned bid, but stipulate that it must be confirmed in writing before the sale starts. On the other hand, it is possible to bid over the telephone at the time of the sale, and many overseas buyers at major auctions do just that, greatly adding to the excitement of the occasion.

It is almost always preferable to bid in person if you possibly can, even though attending sales can be a time-consuming business. It is not always easy to gauge precisely when a particular lot is likely to come up during a sale, and it can be tedious to wait while large numbers of items which have no interest for you are sold. Auctioneers generally sell between 50 and 90 lots per hour, but some are quicker and some slower than this. It is best to ask the advice of a porter or other employee who knows the auctioneer and his speed of selling before planning your movements in and out of the saleroom.

The job lot

One of the problems of buying at auction can be the fact that several items, particularly among the cheaper goods, may be lotted up together. You may only want one or two books from a pile of 20 or 30, or a single drinking glass from an assortment of old and new, chipped, cracked and whole examples. What to do with the dross from these 'job' lots can be a problem, especially if your premises are small. Sometimes you can sort out what you want to keep from several lots and then re-auction the rest. A '£1 and under' box under a fair or market stall, or a junk table outside a shop can take care of a good deal: it is surprising how many people are delighted to rummage about and give small sums for what you might consider useless rubbish. Don't be tempted to throw things away: if you really cannot bear the sight of them, send them to a local jumble sale.

If you are lucky enough to have storage space with your premises—even an attic or an outhouse—you can do worse than keep such unwanted items for a few years. It is surprising what a short time it takes for household oddments to become collectable. Obviously, goods like pictures or textiles must be stored in suitable conditions to prevent deterioration, but 'putting things by' can be a useful precaution for the future.

The ring

A great deal of publicity has been given to the auction-buying skulduggery involving 'rings'. A ring is a group of dealers who agree among themselves not to bid against each other for certain items in a sale but to allow one of their number to bid and, hopefully, secure each for a depressed price. After the sale they have a 'knock-out' or private auction of the objects to decide who finally buys each item and takes it home. Bidding at a knock-out begins at the auction hammer price, and the difference between this and the final knock-out price is then divided between the members of the ring, thus giving them each 'something on the side' as well as the chance of buying goods cheaply. The original buyer or spokesperson is, of course, refunded his outlay.

The practice is totally illegal and there have been several convictions leading to imprisonment for members of rings in recent years. Although rings continue sporadically, it is likely that they will decline gradually, both because of the discouraging example of those convicted and, more effectively, because of the ever-increasing enthusiasm on the part of dealers of integrity and of private individuals who are prepared to pay high prices for the goods they want, and thus prevent rings from being financially worth while. Braving it out against an auction ring can take courage, but persistence is usually rewarded: never be tempted to join one, even if you have friends who do. It is, of course, perfectly legal to buy at auction in partnership with another person or persons, but you should tell the auctioneer beforehand.

Buying from runners

Buying from runners (see page 44) can be highly attractive, since it will save a dealer's own petrol and effort, and often a runner's prices can be pared down to a minimum simply because he has no shop premises and is, presumably, selling quickly after purchase; he has comparatively low overheads and is relying on fast turnover rather than high profit. A clever and experienced runner may build up a good business relationship with several dealers who may come to depend on him for regular supplies of goods. After all, a runner, because he is out on the road so much of the time, often has the ability to track down things that the shop-based dealer could never afford the time to find.

On the other hand, many dealers actively enjoy the hunt for stock and do not relish having items found for them. Others dislike the idea that the runner may have shown a piece to half a dozen rival dealers on the way to his shop. Then it can be embarrassing to get the runner to hump a heavy piece of furniture out of his car or van to examine it and finally decide to reject it. To avoid the feeling of pressure to buy some dealers make a point of never considering goods brought by runners.

Buying privately

A similar awkwardness can arise when a private individual brings in an object in the hope that a dealer will buy it. To begin with, it can be difficult to reject it if it is not suitable: perhaps it is a reproduction piece, or simply has no appeal for the dealer. Then there is invariably a problem over price. If a dealer feels inclined to buy he may ask the person what he or she wants for the item. Naturally, few private individuals have up-to-date knowledge of antique values and therefore most have to ask the dealer to make an offer. Some forget that the dealer must allow himself a profit on the resale and feel disappointed when he offers what they consider a low price. Others distrust him anyway and say they'll 'go away and think about it'; in fact this often means they will go to another dealer (or several) to see if they can get a better offer. They may register surprise if they return to the first dealer and he then refuses to buy, but in the eyes of the trade such actions are not 'cricket', however much one may sympathise with the vendor. If a private individual puts himself in the hands of a dealer by asking him to make an offer for something, it is reasonable to expect the individual to accept or reject the offer there and then.

It is much more satisfactory to buy from established

clients, especially those with whom a dealer may have built up a mutually trusting relationship over a period of time. Many dealers find their clients as valuable in supplying them with stock as in buying goods from them, and it can be to an individual's advantage to sell to a dealer rather than through an auction.

Buying back

Some dealers are happy to buy back from clients goods they have supplied in the past, particularly if they are of high quality. Indeed, there are dealers who rely heavily on being able to buy back former stock. One London dealer in top quality furniture expects to buy back as much as 35 to 40 per cent of the goods his firm has sold, and if he was not able to do this he would be unable to maintain the traditionally high standards of the business.

Beware of stolen goods

In spite of the occasional difficulties, many dealers find it helpful to have goods brought to them for sale. The number of signs on shop doors saying 'Antiques Bought and Sold' or lists of items the dealer wishes to acquire is evidence of the widespread practice of gaining stock in this way. In many cases the dealer is likely to know the person offering goods for sale, particularly in country districts, but it is important that dealers should be awake to the possibility that objects brought in by strangers may be stolen (see page 85).

If you are considering buying from an individual you do not know, it is a wise precaution to ask for his or her name and address and some form of identification. You may also ask him to sign a declaration to the effect that the object is his property to sell. Take the number of his car and be suspicious if you are offered an object at a price much lower than its market value. Such steps may not safeguard you from financial loss if the object turns out to be 'hot' and it is later discovered, but at least you are unlikely to be prosecuted for receiving stolen goods. The following example shows what can happen.

A man went into a London antiques market and offered a clock to one of the dealers, saying it had belonged to his wife's mother, now deceased, and that he and his wife wanted to raise some cash. The dealer was a little suspicious (he did not recognise the man) but was interested in the clock and said he would give him £60 for it; first, however, he would like the man to sign a document affirming his right to sell, and to supply his name and address. He did so, giving an address in the neighbourhood of the antiques market. When the dealer asked for identification the man hesitated, but said he would go and find his driving licence. He returned after some little time and the details of the driving licence tallied with the others he had given to the dealer. The transaction completed, the dealer put the clock on display on his stand.

A few weeks later a lady walked past and surprised the dealer by exclaiming 'Good heavens, there's my clock!' She was able to identify it by a personal inscription on the back, and said it had been stolen from her house nearby, a month or so earlier. The police were called and the dealer produced all the details the man had given him when he sold the clock. When the police visited the man's address they found him at home, and they also found a number of other objects stolen in the same burglary. He was taken to court, and the lady received most of her stolen property back. The dealer, whose care in recording the man's name and details eventually led to justice being done, was not prosecuted for receiving the stolen clock, but he lost the clock and the £60 he had paid for it.

This case had a more satisfactory conclusion than most, but it is obviously difficult to guard against the possibility of a seller of stolen goods giving a false name and address and backing them up with stolen documents. Paying for goods by cheque may be a small safeguard. Acceptance of a cheque by a 'private' seller is usually a good sign: thieves or fences most often demand cash.

If an object that you know has been stolen is offered to you—perhaps it is among the missing items detailed in police circulars to antique dealers—it is obviously helpful if you can alert the police. It may be difficult to keep the would-be seller in the shop while you make a quick telephone call to summon them, but try to gain as much information as possible about the seller and where he or she procured the item in question. Most important and probably most difficult of all, without parting with any money, do your best to hang on to the object itself until the police arrive.

If you see a stolen object in someone else's shop or on a market stall you should also tell the police. Having noted the exact whereabouts of the stolen item, fetch a policeman and return with him to identify it. He is then likely to take possession of it after discovering as much as possible from the shopkeeper or stall-holder about how he acquired it. Obviously, he may be an innocent link in a long chain of owners since the original theft: there is provision in law for ownership disputes to be sorted out in such cases.

Buying abroad

While the majority of dealers confine their searches for stock to their native territory there are some, particularly in certain fields—clocks and scientific instruments, art nouveau and art deco, and antiquities spring to mind—who regularly travel abroad on buying trips. Buying abroad can be fun and provide interesting new fields for exploration, but there are a few pitfalls of which every dealer should beware. The chief concerns the customs regulations for bringing commercial goods into Britain, and these can not only entail long and unproductive hours waiting in dockside customs sheds but can add greatly to the expense of the trip.

To begin with, commercial vehicles are rated higher than others in transport charges, and whether you are using your private car or a large container to bring back your findings, if these are for resale your vehicle must be classed as a commercial one. Second, the procedure for bringing goods into Britain is complicated and the processing and form-filling involved can only be undertaken by a customs agent. Customs agents are private contractors recognised by the Customs and Excise, and they make a considerable charge for their services.

When you arrive back from your trip with your carload of antiques, you must go through the red customs channel whence you will probably be filtered off into a special shed to await customs clearance (with the help of the agent). You will almost certainly find yourself in a queue with other commercial vehicles who may be carrying anything from fruit and vegetables or clothing to heavy machinery. On a good day you may only have to wait four or five hours, but if the queue is long the process may be more lengthy. In America, it is said, these import procedures can take up to five days.

Another aspect of buying abroad concerns the auction habits of other countries. Buying in foreign salerooms should only be undertaken by the experienced or intrepid (but you need to be intrepid to gain the necessary experience). In France, for example, the auction system is positively hair-raising to the uninitiated: there is little opportunity for viewing and several sales are usually conducted simultaneously which makes for considerable confusion; transactions in the salerooms, like those with antique dealers in France, are almost invariably in cash.

Anything purchased in France and described as 'antique' must have a certificate of clearance from the Musée des Beaux Arts in Paris to say that it is not of national importance. Failure to produce a certificate at one of the French channel ports could mean a return trip to Paris!

In Germany and Holland the auction systems are better organised but still somewhat different from our own, and saleroom buying should not be entered into without proper understanding of their rules and habits. This applies to almost any European country.

In the United States the auction procedure is somewhat similar to the British, with the major difference that American auctioneers are more likely than British to be taken to court for misrepresentation if they describe goods as period when they are not. The result is that practically everything in an American sale catalogue is described as 'Queen Anne style' or 'Federal style' just to be on the safe side. For the dealer who really knows what is what, this can sometimes provide bargains. However, shipping costs from America will inevitably add enormously to the price of goods purchased there, and it is unlikely that any but the very experienced and very up-market will make buying forays across the Atlantic.

Incidentally it is never good policy to entrust the shipping of gear to a foreign dealer. For one thing it can lead to an uncontrollable escalation of costs and for another there is little redress if things go wrong. Always use a recognised art and antiques shipping firm if you are not transporting the goods yourself (see page 140).

The final caveat for the would-be buyer abroad concerns the reluctance on the part of many dealers, especially in France, to issue invoices with the goods they sell. Most will only deal in cash anyway and this can present difficulties for the British dealer trying to keep on the correct side of the Inland Revenue and the VAT man.

All this said, buying abroad can still be a fruitful and happy experience. Perhaps the best way for the beginner to approach it would be as an extension to a holiday. It is well worth while looking for bargains in antique and flea markets (practically every major city in Europe has at least one). Because of the vagaries of foreign taste, it can be surprising how many items which are popular and saleable in Britain are misunderstood and virtually disregarded on the continent. It is these 'sleepers'—many of them are likely to be British in origin—which are worth looking for.

While the best examples of anything are likely to fetch most in their country of origin, the less rarefied may be more plentiful and cheaper. For example, a top-quality piece of Lalique glass will almost certainly fetch its top price in France, but because so much Lalique can be found in France, an English dealer may find he can buy the comparatively ordinary examples more favourably than he can at home.

House clearances

Some dealers undertake house clearances as a means of acquiring stock cheaply and, presumably, in the hope of discovering treasures. The system of offering a lump sum for the entire contents of a house may seem attractive. In fact, it can be an unpleasant and unrewarding task in the majority of cases. House clearances are nearly always occasioned by the death of a householder, and may involve clearing soiled bedlinen, stale food in the fridge, grotty carpets and old clothes as well as the furniture and decorative items which are presumably the main attraction. When a dealer makes his offer for a clearance he should make an inventory of the goods: the most attractive objects have a habit of disappearing before the appointed day. If possible, he should arrange to pay after he has done the job.

Chapter 8

Running the Business

Opening hours

What is likely to have a considerable effect on your reputation, and probably therefore your success, is the reliability of your opening hours. Nothing is more exasperating to a potential client than to make a special trip to a dealer's premises only to find it shut for no good reason. It is widely accepted that most antique shops do not open in the morning until 9.30 or 10, that they will be shut for lunch and closed by 5.30 in the evening; it is reasonable to close either on Saturday afternoon or on the local early closing day, but whatever hours you decide to keep, you should make every effort to stick to them. Obviously, you may have to close at other times if your business does not run to a full-time assistant, but in this case it is a good idea to provide a list of opening hours on the door or in the window, so that visitors can plan their trips, and whatever hours you advertise should be punctiliously adhered to. Nothing is more detrimental to a dealer's trade than a reputation (quickly gained) for opening only 'when he feels like it'.

At night it is advisable to leave at least some lights on in the shop, both for security reasons and to encourage window-shoppers. It is surprising how many return to buy after seeing something through the window when the shop is closed.

Pricing

The subject of pricing antiques is a somewhat vexed one: whatever ticket you put on an item, someone is bound to say it is too high, and at the same time there are so many considerations in pricing goods in antique shops that every case has to be treated differently. The old adage that 'an antique is worth what you can get for it' is not much help in determining the actual price-tag to put on an item.

However, there are several points to be borne in mind when pricing stock, and one or two principles will affect your general approach. Few dealers nowadays stick to a standard margin of profit: the idea of adding 30 per cent or 50 per cent (or more), rigidly, to whatever price you paid for an object is against almost all the fundamental notions about antique dealing, and is more or less impracticable in any case.

Some dealers operate on a fast turnover, low profit principle, while others prefer to make a high profit on fewer sales. Much depends on the nature of the business. Obviously if you are a runner with no showroom, or a stall-holder in a weekly market, quick turnover can be the secret of success. A runner who is able to buy a table for £1500 and sell it the same day will be doing well even if his profit is only 10 per cent, and if he can sell several items on quickly after buying them he does not have to worry too much about the size of his profit on each.

There used to be a dealer in Bermondsey market who came each week with completely different stock—boxes full of *bric-à-brac* which he knocked out for the lowest possible prices. People used to stand round his stall and fight for the bargains: he knew they were bargains and that he could sell them for more money if he chose to wait, but he reckoned to sell practically every item he brought in a few hours, and anything unsold at the end of the morning he'd leave behind for the scavengers anyway. He probably made much more money than most of the other dealers who held out for higher profits, and brought back substantially the same stock week after week.

If, on the other hand, you have an expensive showroom where people are not falling over each other to buy up your stock, you will expect to sell fewer items— maybe only one or two things each week—and your profit margin must be considerably higher. The table you buy from the runner for £1650 may sit in your shop for two or three months before you sell it, and the profit you eventually make must reflect this. Taking this principle to the extreme, it is not unknown for an antique dealer to make a handsome living by selling only one or two items a year.

What people are prepared to pay for antiques is enormously affected by the prestige of the premises in which they are found. Coolly displayed in the grand showrooms of Bond Street are price tags which would be laughable in the majority of antique shops, and dealers are sometimes shocked to discover fine and rare items they have sold to other dealers marked up to what they consider absurd and extortionate levels. In truth, they probably would be absurd in their shops, but in these exalted halls they are the norm. The fact is that some people, especially rich private buyers, are prepared to pay enormously inflated prices for high quality items in reassuringly prestigious surroundings. Indeed, they are likely to be suspicious of anything less than very expensive: it is as if the high price is a guarantee of genuineness as well as quality. Many dealers can tell of 'stickers' they have sold immediately by the simple expedient of doubling the figure on the price ticket. Another solution is to move them into a different part of the shop.

Even on a less exalted level, what you have paid for an item may have little to do with the price you sell it for. Obviously, when you are buying you will do your best to find things which you consider are under-priced or at least worth more than you are paying for them; by how much will be very variable. Sometimes you may buy something you rate highly for quite a low price. Naturally, you will mark it with a price tag in keeping with your own estimate of its worth, even if that represents a high percentage of profit. Conversely, you may pay 'over the odds' for an item you like very much, knowing that there is little or no profit left in it. In that case you will have to be prepared to sell it for a narrow margin.

There may even be occasions when you decide to sell at a loss: if you have had an object a long time and it is clearly too highly priced, it may be more useful to realise whatever cash you can from it than to have your capital tied up in unsaleable merchandise.

Just to keep things moving in this way, some dealers have an occasional clear-out and send a few lots to the saleroom where they may or may not sell well, but at least they will bring in some money which can be spent more profitably.

Unless you are the kind of dealer who relies solely on speed of turnover it is unwise to sell too hastily. Anyone will tell you that a dealer's chief problem is in finding stock, not selling it. If you buy something you like but do not know much about, it is nearly always worth spending a bit of time on research. You may find you have something even more interesting than you had at first thought, and the more you find out about a piece, the greater your chance of selling it for a good price. Selling something to the first person who offers you a few bob profit may be heartily regretted later, when it is too late. Have confidence in your purchases, and if you rate a piece highly, don't be pressured into selling it too quickly. The chances are that sooner or later someone will come along who can appreciate it too, and be willing to part with their money for its full worth.

Price guides

The usefulness—or otherwise—of price guides to antiques has been debated long and hard. For some people, particularly those new to the trade, they can be helpful in providing the most basic guidance, so long as they are not taken too literally. Many are illustrated with line drawings rather than photographs, and most of the prices quoted are for typical auction results; as these fluctuate drastically and as practically every antique is different, not only in form and style but also as regards condition and provenance, price guiding is a notoriously inexact science. The more useful of them are probably the specialised publications: such subjects as fairings, pot lids, corkscrews and Stevengraphs can more accurately be assessed than the publishers of volumes on the prices of pottery and porcelain, furniture, or even the whole field of antiques, would have us believe.

Back numbers (not too far back) of trade papers such as *Antiques Trade Gazette* are probably more worth studying than most price guides, and are certainly more up to date. Regular reading of such publications is undoubtedly valuable in building up a general knowledge of prices realised by art and antiques at auction.

In the end, pricing of antiques really comes down to experience. By degrees you will learn what you can expect to sell something for in your particular shop or area, and you will also gain confidence in your judgements and know when you can set a high price on something of good quality.

Trade prices
It is customary among dealers to have a two-tier pricing system: a price to retail customers and a 'trade' price, generally about 10 per cent below the retail price. But, unlike prices for most other commodities, even these are not usually fixed, and both retail and trade customers generally expect to haggle over the prices they pay for goods. While a dealer will probably reduce the price a little for a retail or 'private' customer, he is unlikely to go as low as the trade price. From another dealer he may accept a still lower figure than his trade price, and in this case, much will depend on the circumstances—who the dealer is, whether he is a regular and valued customer, whether he is buying several items and, of course, how keen the dealer is to make a sale.

Labelling
Having decided on the price you are going to ask for an item, it should be labelled clearly. A full description of the piece, its approximate date, the retail price and the stock number are usually included, and the trade price may be added in code. This may simply take the form of adding a number to the price figure, ie, a trade price of £38 may be written 638; or it may involve substituting letters for figures, or turning the figures back to front and prefixing or suffixing them with another number: every dealer develops his own system. Most of these codes are easily deciphered

by the experienced, and it hardly matters: most dealers will regard the label price merely as a starting point from which to begin bargaining.

Good labelling gives confidence to potential purchasers and at the same time obviates the need for constant questions while they are browsing. Visitors should be able to gain as much information as possible from looking at the goods themselves and their labels, and they will prefer not to have to ask prices. Some dealers will, of course, disagree with this, and suggest that labels can come between the dealer and his customers, cutting out any reason for discussion, but they are in a minority.

Whatever you do, check your price tags: if an item is incorrectly labelled, say for too little, and somebody buys the piece for the wrong price, there is nothing you can do. Once money has changed hands, you cannot go back to the buyer and say that you inadvertently left a nought off the price tag: the piece is legally his, for the price he paid (see page 84).

A practical point: tie-on labels are preferable to stick-on, which can not only damage objects all too easily but can be switched from one to another by the dishonest.

Researching

There are many ways of delving into the origins of an item. You may find useful reference material in appropriate books or periodicals and it is always worth the time spent keeping up your own reference system, particularly if you are a specialist. A card index giving details of magazine and newspaper articles on particular subjects, catalogues and illustrations, as well as information about items you have seen or owned in the past (with or without photographs) can be invaluable in filling out the background to acquisitions. Auction catalogues and price-lists constitute especially useful reference material, particularly if they have a large number of illustrations.

Museum expertise can be sought for objects of noteworthy interest. Nearly every museum makes provision for visitors to bring in items for opinion and, while valuations are not given, other useful historical information is often forthcoming.

Legal angles

It is every antique dealer's nightmare that an incompetent assistant will take an object out of the window priced at £150 and sell it for £1.50; or that he or she will mark an item at £1.50 when it should be £150. The question arises of what redress you have in such circumstances.

The Sale of Goods Act

The law over this and many other matters with which dealers come into contact is governed by the Sale of Goods Act. For instance, in the case of the specific example given, once money has changed hands between a seller (or his/her agent, in this case an employee) and a buyer, a bargain has been struck and there is no going back on it. On the other hand, the display of goods in a shop, even with a price clearly marked on them is an 'invitation to treat', not an 'offer to sell'. A buyer cannot insist that you sell the goods at the price marked on them.

However, once an offer has been made and accepted, a contract between buyer and seller has been established. Like all contracts, though, it can be voided if it can be shown to be defective or illegal. One common cause of that in the antique business is misrepresentation on the seller's part. If a seller describes a chair as being eighteenth century and of the Hepplewhite period and it turns out to be an Edwardian copy, that is misrepresentation. Misrepresentation can be innocent — in the antique trade this is often the case. But it can also be intentional, in which case it is fraudulent and liable for criminal prosecution. In either case the contract is void and you would have to give the buyer his money back. Some dealers, in fact, offer to do so automatically if an attribution they make turns out to be wrong, or even if the buyer has good reason to think it might be so.

The other frequent cause of a contract being void is

if the article in question turns out to be stolen. In that case you would have to return it to its owner and you would lose whatever you had paid for it, even if you had come by it honestly. Otherwise, of course, you would face prosecution for a criminal offence as well. It is possible to insure against this happening, providing it was done innocently. There is, however, a curious loophole here. If you acquire the item in what is called a 'market overt'—that is an open air market—in good faith that the seller has a rightful title to it, then you have a right of ownership even if it subsequently turns out to have been stolen. This does not, however, apply in Scotland.

A further reason why a contract might be void is if the goods in question are sold in breach of the Trade Descriptions Acts. These require the seller to give a true description of what he is offering and for this reason it is important to be very careful about the wording in catalogues, advertisements, or other bits of literature which contain descriptions of items you are selling or buying.

Once the bargain has been completed, though, the buyer must remove the goods from your premises—the same applies to you if you are the buyer, obviously—within a reasonable period of time. If they fail to do so you are entitled to charge them for safekeeping.

The goods must also be paid for in full, within a reasonable time. If this does not happen, the seller may have the right to resell them, but the situation becomes very tricky if he has accepted part payment. If no money has changed hands it is always possible to argue that no bargain has been struck, but that would be a difficult line to take if a part payment had been accepted. You could, if you were the seller, warn the buyer verbally or in writing that you would resell the goods unless they were collected by a certain date, but unless the buyer agreed to that, you might find it difficult to make it stick. Silence, in law, is not accepted as a sign of agreement with whatever proposition was being put.

Another problem that sometimes comes up is when a prospective buyer is allowed to take goods away to see if they fit into a decorative scheme at home. This has been known to happen with items such as carpets. If the person concerned hangs on to them for an un-reasonable period of time, he or she is regarded in law as having effectively agreed to buy the item or items concerned. However, until that point is reached, they remain the property of the intending seller. Should they be damaged or stolen while they are with the prospective buyer, it is the former who has to bear the loss. Again, it is possible to insure against this circumstance but as a general rule it is never a good idea to let people take away goods without payment in full, unless you are absolutely sure of their *bona fides*.

Auctions

Auctioneers are very conscious of the implications of the Trade Descriptions Acts in the wording of their catalogues—hence the importance of understanding the terminology they use (see page 66). They must also give bidders the opportunity to examine the goods before they are put up for sale. Once a bid is made it is regarded as an offer to purchase—and a bargain is struck at the fall of the hammer. From that point on, the goods become your property and you are responsible for such matters as insurance.

In auctions, too, there are circumstances where a sale is voided. One is if you can prove that a ring has been in operation; a situation discussed on pages 69-70. It is also illegal for the seller to bid on his or her own behalf, unless they announce their prior intention to do so.

County courts

Legal actions are always expensive and somehow turn out to be so even if you win. For this reason it is important to try to avoid them as we have indicated, by never parting with goods without getting either cash, or a cleared cheque or credit card payment. Sometimes, if a defaulting customer is unwilling to pay, a solicitor's letter will do the trick. Certainly, if the customer has the means to do so he is likely to pay those who threaten to sue more rapidly than those who simply send reminders not backed up by any stronger action.

Ultimately, though, you may have to resort to action through the county court, which looks after claims for less than £500. The procedure is that you apply for a 'default summons' to your nearest county court and send it in, together with the court fee and details of your claim. This is cheaper than the full panoply of a civil action for the recovery of debt, but it still takes time, money and legal fees. Furthermore, you need to make sure that the debtor really is in a position to pay you. There is no point in pursuing a man of straw; which only goes to show that one shop antique you might invest in is one of those jokey signs which say IN GOD WE TRUST—NO CREDIT GIVEN.

Stolen cheques and cheque cards

While a dealer can take a good many precautions against stolen cheques, there is very little he can do once he finds he has been 'done' with one. He should therefore take every step he can to avoid them. If a stranger wants to buy an item and pay by cheque, the first thing to do is to watch him sign it. Never accept a pre-signed cheque unless you ask him to sign the back as well: it is very difficult for anyone convincingly to forge a signature under the beady eye of another. Then look carefully at the cheque itself, to ensure that it is not a forgery. If necessary compare it with other cheques in the till and see that it conforms in every detail of format and design with other cheques from the same bank.

Ask to see the client's cheque card even if he is buying something for more than £50, and compare the signature of the cheque with that of the cheque card. Be suspicious if he hands you the card in a plastic wallet. Remove the card and examine it carefully. If the signature strip has been tampered with, the word 'void' may appear in the background. The moulded numbers on the front may have been sliced off the surface and others fixed on, in which case the indentations on the back of the cheque card will not conform to the numbers visible on the front.

If the cheque and the cheque card seem genuine enough, you may safeguard yourself by ringing the client's bank to make sure he really has an account. If you do this, find the number and make the call yourself: an old trick is for a villain to give the number of a coin box down the road where his mate is waiting to answer as if he were a bank employee.

However far above suspicion your unknown client appears to be, always take his name and address, and his car registration number if possible. If he seems to be in a hurry, and arrives just before closing time, it is reasonable to question his motives. Remember, anyone buying an item honestly should not mind your enquiries and should welcome your scrupulous attention to his cheque and bank card.

Value added tax (VAT)

Though it is described as a tax, VAT is actually administered and collected by Customs and Excise, not by the Inland Revenue; and if your annual turnover is more than £20,500 (or £7000 in any one quarter) you will have to register with them as a taxable trader. You can also, if you wish, elect to become a taxable trader even if your turnover does not reach these levels. This means that you will have to remit to Customs and Excise, every quarter, 15 per cent of the price you charge on your 'outputs'; that is to say, your sales and any other services you provide and charge for, such as restoration and valuation.

However, you will be able to deduct from those remittances any VAT which you yourself have been charged by your suppliers—your 'inputs'. This means, not only the VAT element on goods and services (again like restoration and valuation) you have bought, but also on everything which you have to buy to run your business—telephone charges, the VAT on petrol and so forth.

Some people find it advantageous to elect for VAT-able status, in spite of the fact that making quarterly VAT returns and keeping detailed records of sales and purchases to support them is an onerous administrative chore. They find it worth while because of the

VAT they are able to recover on their purchases. Others go to considerable lengths to avoid it, even to the extent of trading as two different companies from the same address in order to avoid hitting the £20,500 turnover ceiling which makes registration compulsory.

When VAT was first introduced it was soon pointed out that the antique trade faced special problems. Since sellers outside the trade were not usually registered for VAT, it meant there was no input tax to set off against VAT outputs and that left traders with huge VAT bills to pay. The other point was that it was a tax on services and manufactured goods and that antiques did not fall under that category.

For this reason a 'special scheme' was introduced to cover second-hand works of art, antiques and scientific collections; antiques, for this purpose, were defined as items more than 100 years old. The special scheme is explained, though with less than crystal clarity, in Customs and Excise Notice 712. In essence it says that even though you will have to register for VAT if your turnover reaches the level indicated above, tax is chargeable only *on the margin* between the buying and the selling price—provided the person you sell it to does not claim the tax/VAT element as an input on *his* return. How this can be ascertained is not entirely clear—presumably Customs and Excise make spot checks on the VAT returns of those who have purchased antiques. Certainly, dealers are required to keep very detailed stock books of all the articles which they buy or intend to sell under the scheme—details of what is required in the way of documentation are given in Notice 712. If you operate the special scheme and buy goods from someone who does not issue an invoice, you will have to prepare an invoice on their behalf certifying that they have not claimed VAT on the goods sold under that invoice; you will also have to keep full records of everything bought at auction.

Another point that is not clear is how exactly you know if the goods are more than 100 years old unless there is a hallmark or other datable marking; or indeed how the Customs and Excise VAT inspectors, who are not usually trained art historians, can tell the difference between an object made in 1880 and one made in 1900. Some dealers reportedly describe everything they sell as an antique more than 100 years old, unless it is obviously otherwise: the same information, presumably, which they dispense to their less well-informed customers, who at any rate do not have to pay VAT on the full value of the goods.

Hallmarking
According to the Hallmarking Act 1973, dealers selling articles of gold, silver or platinum of any age must display the official hallmarking sign which describes the approved hallmarks and indicates that all articles on sale are correctly hallmarked. The sign is available from the British Hallmarking Council, PO Box 47, Birmingham B3 2RP.

Packing and shipping

A proportion of almost any antique dealer's trade is inevitably with buyers from abroad. How high a number depends on the nature of the business, but the services of packers and shippers are bound to be needed sooner or later. While buyers of small objects will probably be able to take them in their luggage, trade buyers or purchasers of large items like furniture will have to have them sent separately.

The packaging of antiques for sending abroad is a highly skilled and specialised business, and it is one that should only be undertaken by accredited packers and shippers for the art and antiques trade. Most of these specialist freight firms are based in London but, through a network of agents, they provide their services all over the country; many have branches in major cities throughout the world. A list of them is supplied on page 140. Not only do they take care of the packing of precious and fragile objects safely and securely but they deal with the customs and can go through the export licence procedure on a dealer's behalf (see page 92). If necessary, they can arrange warehousing at either end. Some will even undertake personal travel arrangements among their services.

If your client requires an estimate for packing and shipping, you will need to ring the shipping company, giving the dimensions of the items to be sent as well as the exact destination. Once the go-ahead has been given, you send the shipper the invoice for the articles and the address to which they must be sent, and he will then arrange collection of the goods.

While many buyers from abroad have long-established contacts with particular shippers and will ask you to arrange freight through a specific firm, others will ask your advice in the matter. Experience will inevitably enable you to discover which shipper suits your needs best for price, service and location, and it is likely that you will find yourself using the same firm again and again.

Export of works of art

The rules governing the export of works of art from Britain are laid down by Act of Parliament, and while their finer details will have little relevance for most antique dealers most of the time, everyone concerned in the sale of antiques should be conversant with their basic principles. An export licence is needed for the following categories:

1. Photographic positives and negatives produced more than 60 years before the date of exportation and valued at £400 or more per item.
2. Antiques or collectors' items over 50 years old worth more than £16,000 'per article or matching set of articles', unless they have been imported into Britain within the last 50 years.
3. Documents, manuscripts and archives.
4. Articles recovered from the soil of the United Kingdom or from the seabed in United Kingdom territorial waters after being buried for more than 50 years (except coin).
5. Representations (two- or three-dimensional) of 'British historical personages' (that means anyone listed in the *Dictionary of National*

Biography, Who's Who or *Who Was Who*) with a value of more than £16,000. Items in this category worth between £4000 and £16,000 may only be exported if they are accompanied by a certificate from the Director of the National Portrait Gallery or the Scottish National Portrait Gallery stating that, in his opinion, the object concerned is not of national importance.

A dealer sending abroad a consignment of antiques, none of which requires a specific export licence, must submit a declaration to that effect to the Customs and Excise with the shipping documents. For items requiring a licence the dealer must apply for the appropriate forms to the Department of Trade and Industry, Export Licensing Branch, Millbank Tower, Millbank, London SW1P 4QU. The objects concerned are then referred by the Department of Trade to the appropriate expert adviser (almost invariably a specialist from a major museum) to see whether or not they are of such national importance that they should not leave Britain. The expert may raise no objection to the export, in which case it will be allowed to go ahead, or he may recommend that an export licence be refused because of its national importance. In this case it will be referred to the Reviewing Committee on the Export of Works of Art.

This small but august body will consider the case in the light of three criteria recommended in the Waverley Report of 1952 and since adopted as guidelines in the granting or withholding of export licences for works of art. The Waverley criteria are:

1. Is the object so closely connected with our history and national life that its departure would be a misfortune?
2. Is it of outstanding aesthetic importance?
3. Is it of outstanding significance for the study of some particular branch of art, learning or history?

Depending on how high the object rates in one or

more of these categories the Committee may recommend that an export licence be withheld for a specified period (three or six months is usual) to give a British public collection the opportunity to purchase it. If, at the end of this time, no institution has made the necessary offer (usually because of insufficient funds), the item may be given an export licence. If the owner refuses an offer from a public collection an indefinite embargo may be placed on the item—but this is a rare occurrence.

Every dealer should be in possession of a copy of the regulations. These are laid out in the *Notice to Exporters* which is also available from the Department of Trade and Industry, Export Licensing Branch, Millbank Tower, Millbank, London SW1P 4QU.

Valuations

Many dealers, as well as auctioneers and specialist valuers, undertake valuations for insurance, probate and other purposes as part of their work. No specific qualifications are necessary, but obviously institutions like insurance companies will be less inclined to question valuations given by individuals with some sort of accreditation: membership of the BADA or LAPADA is probably as widely recognised in this respect as membership of a professionally qualifying body like the Incorporated Society of Valuers and Auctioneers or the Royal Institution of Chartered Surveyors. However, valuation by any established antique dealer in a specialised category is usually acceptable in practice.

The most usual reasons for valuations are insurance—in which the valuation is based on the cost of replacing an object—and probate, a lower estimate, based on the price an item would be likely to fetch if sold. The fees charged for valuations vary a good deal. Some individuals charge a time-based flat rate regardless of the total value of the goods involved while the majority charge a percentage of the total valuation according to a sliding scale which goes down as the valuation mounts. For example, the first £10,000 of a valuation may be charged at 1½ per cent, while the next £40,000 will be charged at 1 per cent and all succeeding sums at ½ per cent.

Bearing in mind that no one can know everything, and most dealers, however general, have blank areas of interest in which their knowledge is minimal, valuations should only be undertaken within a dealer's own field of experience. A specialist silver and jewellery dealer, for example, should recommend that a client finds another specialist valuer for furniture or ceramics, and this individual may well decline to value pictures. There is nothing wrong in this: a full valuation conducted by a single individual should be regarded with a certain amount of suspicion.

Restoration

It is most unlikely that everything you buy will be in perfect condition, and sooner or later you will find yourself in need of a restorer of some sort. While there is now no shortage of restorers, really good craftsmen are not so easy to find, and their skills will always be in heavy demand. Some dealers, especially at the top end of the market, employ a full-time restorer on or near their premises; some even maintain workshops occupying several craftsmen covering a whole range of skills. Certainly, it can be a great advantage, especially for a furniture dealer, to have a restorer continually available.

However, such is the variety of restoration skills to be called upon by all but the most specialised dealers, that the majority prefer to call upon the services of freelance workers, some of whom may in fact be dealers as well. The grapevine is probably the best way to discover these craftsmen, but you may have to shop around for a while before you discover those that particularly suit your needs. It is as well to remember that the cheapest may not be the most inexpensive in the long run: it is said that more damage is done to antique furniture by bad restoration than by any amount of wear and tear, and the same is probably true of most other antiques, particularly pictures and textiles.

This is also worth bearing in mind if you decide to

embark on your own repairs. While much can be done to improve an item by cleaning and/or polishing, do-it-yourself restoration should only be undertaken for superficial and straightforward problems. A working knowledge of cabinet-making and other technical skills is obviously a great advantage to a dealer. While he may not have the time, inclination or necessary level of expertise to carry out his own restoration, he will be in a much better position to assess the time and materials involved (and therefore the cost) in repairing a damaged piece, and this can be of vital importance in estimating how much he can afford to pay for it in the first place.

If you undertake to have a client's furniture restored, it is important first to get a detailed estimate from the craftsman who is to do the work. Private individuals who do not fully comprehend the time involved in restoration are often horrified at the cost, and they must be given the chance to accept or refuse an estimate for repairs before the restorer is given the go-ahead.

Photography

A photographic record of every item that passes through their hands is a luxury few dealers can afford, although it can be of inestimable interest and usefulness. For basic records such as this, polaroid prints are adequate and they can be produced almost instantly. These can also be invaluable for sending through the post to possible clients (see page 113).

If pictures are required for publicity and advertising it is worth having good quality photographs taken—by a professional if you are not an expert photographer yourself. It is said that one good black and white photograph can do more to sell a piece than 1000 words written about it, and the expense involved should be regarded as an investment. It is worth remembering that the main cost of photography, at least in black and white, lies in setting up and taking the first shot: duplicate prints are comparatively inexpensive, and it is a good idea to order plenty of extra ones. They can be useful for all sorts of purposes—publicity, stock records and security to name a few.

Keep your photographs in an organised way, in a filing cabinet under subjects, or in folders, so that they can be retrieved easily. Above all, caption them before putting them away; in a few years' time you may have forgotten the details of the piece, and a photograph without a description of what it portrays is virtually useless. A caption should always include the visual details, period attribution and provenance of an item, and if possible, measurements, but the more information you can muster about its background history, comparative examples, how much you paid for it, who bought it, and so on, the more interesting the photograph becomes as a record in later years.

Finding a professional photographer should not be difficult. While the handful of specialists in art and antique photography are almost all to be found in London, the average town has at least one photographic studio capable of producing reasonably good 'still-life' work, whether this is for the antiques trade or for industrial and other commercial purposes. If a photographer is not customarily involved with antiques it is essential to brief him thoroughly about your need, or even to supervise the shot in person. You must tell him the angle from which you want the item photographed; if appropriate, whether it is to be open or shut; whether you want the details of decoration to be the main focus, or the form of the piece itself: until you know your photographer well, do not assume that he automatically knows what you want.

Better (and cheaper) results will be generally obtained if you can take items to the studio to be photographed, but for large objects the photographer will have to visit your premises. Much can be done to clarify background with wide rolls of smooth paper—sheets of material are best avoided: they are invariably creased.

Still-life photography in colour is, of course, more expensive than black and white, and for many purposes it may not hold great advantages. If, however, you are wanting a photograph to demonstrate a highly

colourful item—like a piece of porcelain or an embroidery—you will almost certainly require colour. While
the best results are obtained with transparencies of
at least 3 by 4 inches (for which the photographer
needs a special plate camera), smaller transparencies,
2¼ inches square, can be nearly as good. Magazine
and other reproductions can even be made from 35mm
transparencies if the definition is good enough, but
the larger sizes are preferable. Modern methods of
printing allow colour prints to be used for reproduction
in many instances, but these must also be of the highest quality and of a minimum size.

Computers

The use of computer systems in the art and antiques
world is still in its infancy but, however resistant
dealers may be to the idea, it is likely that they will
persist and proliferate over the next few years. One
system, designed by an antique dealer especially for
dealers, is that of Antony Sidgwick, 25 Park Street,
Cirencester, Gloucestershire (0285 68676). This can
be used with any standard business machine and
replaces stock books, keeps accounts and includes
customer mailing and customer interest sections.
Clearly, by taking so much of the drudgery out of
administration, computer systems can give dealers
much more time to concentrate on dealing.

Children

Dealers are often nervous of children coming into
their shops, but they should not be. The children are
usually there either because they themselves have an
interest in antiques or because their parents have, in
which case they are likely to be used to living with fragile objects. Most children over the age of six are quite
capable of looking without having to touch everything,
and in any case they are generally much less liable
to cause damage than carelessly carried handbags.

Very small children can be a liability, but wise and
welcoming proprietors should try to divert them
with something interesting and pretty, and give their

parents a chance to relax and look round the shop. A really enlightened child-orientated dealer, like the owners of certain other shops nowadays, will even keep a few objects especially for children to play with, and this can do nothing but encourage their parents to feel welcome and, above all, to buy.

Many children of seven or eight and upwards show a marked interest in the past and in collecting. A small table or section of inexpensive objects can be very attractive to them. Children should always be encouraged: they are the collectors of tomorrow.

Keeping accounts

Every business ought to keep accounts and, if it is set up as a limited company or if it is registered for VAT—which it will have to be if its turnover exceeds a figure laid down in each year's Finance Act, there is a legal obligation to do so. Many people running antique shops get round the problem of what is often a temperamental disinclination to keep accounts by getting a freelance book-keeper to do it for them. Your accountant will probably be able to recommend the services of such a person. Indeed, if you intend to do it this way it is in any case advisable to consult your accountant at an early stage, so that he or she can lay down how the books should be kept.

In actual fact, for a small business the procedures are not very complicated and it helps if you understand something of them yourself whatever course of action you decide to adopt regarding book-keeping. The most basic records consist of the following.

Cash book

This simply records income and expenditure: income goes on the left-hand side of a double-page spread, expenditure on the right-hand side. Each side is ruled off vertically to give essential details of the transactions that are entered—the date, the description of what was sold (or purchased), the relevant cheque or credit card number, the invoice number if any, the cost and the amount of VAT involved.

Some of these transactions may be purely in cash,

others will be in the form of cheques or credit cards. For instance, you may be paying by cheque in an auction, but paying a runner in cash; or taking a cheque from a dealer but selling for cash to casual customers. The important thing is to keep a record of every sale or purchase and enter the details in the book daily. You must record payments you make into the business's bank account and also withdrawals for purposes other than paying for goods. Your accountant will show you how to do this. He will also probably suggest that, as a double check, you should get monthly statements from the bank showing all transactions. For a small extra charge you can get a more detailed statement than the normal one. Credit card companies also provide a detailed statement, which is why it is a good idea to use a credit card for purchase transactions that fall between those that can readily be dealt with in cash and those that are generally paid for by cheque.

Petty cash book
For minor cash transactions it is advisable to keep a petty cash book. This simply records small sums that are paid out of or into the till: postage, taxis and so forth on the expenditure side; or sales from the 'anything on this shelf under £1' display that many shops have.

Wages book
If you employ staff you will also need to keep a wages book. This shows for each person their gross earnings, deductions for tax, National Insurance contributions, net pay and the employer's NI contribution. You will have to learn the formulae under which PAYE is deducted. Your accountant or tax office will show you what to do.

Other books of account
If you buy or sell goods on credit—for instance if you have an account with a regular supplier, or regular customers have an account with you—book-keeping becomes rather more complicated. You will then need a sales day book and a purchase day book for recording

invoices: also sales and purchase ledgers with pages allotted to individual customers or suppliers. This takes you deep into the mysteries and complications of double-entry book-keeping, but fortunately very few small antique shops are operated on a credit basis.

Profit and loss account

From the information provided in these books, your accountant will draw together the figures needed to compile your profit and loss account: the vital function of which is to tell you whether you have been making a profit or a loss in your trading over a given period. It can be monthly, quarterly, annual or over whatever segment of time is likely to show a significant picture. In the case of businesses registered for VAT it should be done at least quarterly, though there is no direct connection between VAT and profitability. VAT has to be paid on turnover, irrespective of whether you are making a loss or a profit.

To compile the profit and loss figure you deduct from the sales figure over the period chosen, the value of opening stock at the beginning of the period, plus purchases during it *less* the value of closing stock: that gives you a gross profit. From that you further deduct all your overheads, rent, repairs, travel and so forth, to arrive at a net profit figure.

Profit and Loss Account for month of...

	£	£
Sales	—	2,000
Opening stock	300	
Purchases	600	900
Gross profit		1,100
Rent and rates	100	
Travel	55	
Phone	34	
Heat and light	63	
Repairs	123	
Professional fees	45	
		420
Net profit		680

An important factor in establishing your profit and loss position at the end of the tax year, and one which particularly affects the antiques business is the valuation of your stock. Inevitably you will find yourself with slow moving items and those which, for one reason or another, are worth less than you paid for them. Accepting this unwelcome fact will reduce your profitability, but it is important to be realistic about write-downs because this will reduce your tax bill. You are compounding your error if you put yourself in the position of paying tax on mythical profits.

The balance sheet
If you are set up as a limited company your accountant will have to produce a balance sheet at the end

Balance Sheet as at 31.12.86

	£	£	£	£
Fixed Assets				
Vehicles	1,600			
less depreciation	400		1,200	
Fixtures and fittings	1,000			
less depreciation	250		750	
			1,950	
Current Assets				
Stock	3,000			
Debtors	900			
Cash	75			
		3,975		
Less Current Liabilities				
Trade Creditors		795		
Net Current Assets			3,180	
Total Assets			5,130	

	Authorised	Issued
Represented by		
Capital (1,000 shares at £1 each)	1,000	500
Loan repayable 1986		1,000
Profit		3,630
		5,130

of your financial year and lodge it with the Registrar of Companies. The balance sheet is generally described as a snapshot, taken at a given *point of time*, of what a company *owes* and what it *owns*. This is different from the profit and loss account, which simply sets out the trading position over a *period* of time.

The balance sheet is divided between fixed and current assets and liabilities. In the case of assets, the fixed ones are those which are permanently necessary to the conduct of the business—a car or van bought in the name of the company, your lease, fittings and so forth. The current ones are those that can be easily realised—stock, amounts owed to you by debtors, and, obviously, cash at the bank.

With liabilities, the position is reversed. The fixed ones are those which you do not have to repay immediately like a bank loan. You do, however, have to pay the interest on the loan, so that is a current liability, as are any debts you owe. The profit from the trading account is also a liability, because it is a debt owed to the shareholders. Losses on the balance sheet are deducted from previously retained profits or, if there are no retained profits, from the shareholders' capital.

What you can learn from your accounts
The *total liabilities*, deducted from the *total assets* on your balance sheet will give you the amount of capital employed in your business. Assuming you are making a profit, one of the things you will probably want to know is whether you are getting a better return from the capital employed than if you invested it in other ways. The formula for that is:

$$\frac{Profit}{Capital\ employed} \times 100$$

If you are getting less than a 10 per cent return on your capital and you are having to pay yourself out of that percentage you may have to take steps to improve the profitability of the business by increasing prices or expanding the range of your activities.

You also ought to make sure that your current

assets are greater than your current liabilities. Otherwise, if a major current liability is called in unexpectedly, you may have a financial crisis on your hands. There are many other kinds of ratios that can be applied to test whether or not your business is in good shape. For instance:

$$\frac{\text{Sales}}{\text{Cost of sales}} \times 100$$

determines your profit percentage. Which ratios are the crucial ones to watch depends somewhat on the nature of your trading. An antique business, for instance, should be particularly interested in how quickly the stock is turned over. You should ask your accountant's advice on the ratios you need to watch most closely.

Selling your own possessions

Most people regard tax as being a fairly cut and dried matter but in fact a good deal of what is and is not liable is left to the discretion of individual tax inspectors. A case in point is whether putting your personal possessions into stock makes you liable for tax on the profits when they are sold. Some tax inspectors have taken the view that this is a trading transaction and that such disposals do not therefore qualify as a capital gain, on which relief would otherwise be given up to a maximum of £6300 (1986 figure). Others appear to take a more lenient view. What is clear, though, is that if you intend to put privately collected objects in as stock in trade, you should get them independently valued first in order to arrive at a profit figure from which the tax can be calculated.

Chapter 9
Employing Staff

Like parenthood, employing people immediately involves you in a mass of legislation and a whole range of constraints; and to a very large extent there is virtually no distinction between the obligations of a major employer and one with only a single employee.

Employing an assistant

If you have a shop or gallery you will almost certainly need to employ an assistant, at least part-time, unless you are in partnership. Some people are lucky enough to have help from a member of the family and this often means that working arrangements can be more flexible than is possible with a formally employed assistant.

On the other hand, many dealers prefer to have a reliable assistant on a regular basis so that they can organise their buying trips and other outside business in a predictable fashion without having to worry too much about the running of the shop. Indeed, some dealers, blessed with an experienced and dependable assistant, will leave the management of the showroom almost entirely to him or her and become effectively peripatetic, travelling in search of new stock, visiting restorers, viewing sales, making valuations and dealing with the many other outside concerns that crop up.

Honesty and punctuality are perhaps the most obvious qualities needed by an antique dealer's assistant; enthusiasm, discretion and personal charm are also important, and command of other languages, secretarial and book-keeping skills may be added bonuses. While experience with antiques and enthusiasm are a distinct advantage in an assistant, beware of the over-ambitious. To begin with, such an employee will have little incentive to remain for any length of time, and second, you may find his or her interest in working for you is limited to what you can provide in the way of knowledge or contacts. At least one specialist dealer has discovered a temporary assistant busy copying out her address list of collectors as a preliminary step in his own dealing career—a particularly brazen form of poaching.

However, a young assistant who is keen to learn and takes the trouble to read and do research can be an asset in any business and the dealer should keep such interest alive by sharing his or her knowledge and being as encouraging as possible. Lack of such stimulation by the dealer is likely to lead to a sense of exclusion on the part of an assistant, who is then more likely to leave.

A great many dealers employ older assistants, especially if they require only part-time help. Mature women tend to be reliable in these types of position, and while they may be knowledgeable and experienced, they tend not to suffer from restless ambition on their own account.

It is also worth bearing in mind that the administrative costs of hiring part-timers are much less, provided that their weekly remuneration falls below the level at which the employer must deduct PAYE—at present £35.50 a week. That eliminates the dreaded PAYE paperwork and also removes the employer's liability to make the statutory National Insurance contribution of 10.45 per cent of salary per employee.

You have to be careful, on the other hand, of part-timers earning over that amount but who claim to be freelancers making their own tax and NI arrangements as Schedule D taxpayers. The Inland Revenue have narrowed their definitions here and would be unlikely to recognise their independent status. In such a case you might be liable for any PAYE and NI deductions that you had failed to make.

The contract of employment

Even those who are working part-time are covered by contracts of employment. Whole books could be and have been written about the legal technicalities of the subject, but for practical purposes all you need to know are the major pitfalls you should look out for when you start employing people.

The contract of employment statement which has to be issued in writing to every employee who is going to work for you for 16 hours or more per week within 13 weeks of joining is in fact not a pitfall, but a rather sensible document which clarifies right from the outset what the terms of employment are. From the employer's point of view, the necessity of drafting a contract of employment statement should concentrate the mind wonderfully on issues about which it is all too easy to be sloppy at the expense of subsequent aggravation, such as hours of work, holidays and, above all, exactly what it is the employee is supposed to be doing. The following points have to be covered in the contract, and you must say if you have not covered one or other of them:

- The rate of pay and how it is calculated
- Whether it is paid weekly or monthly
- The normal hours of work and the terms and conditions relating to them
- Holidays and holiday pay
- Provision for sick pay
- Pension and pension schemes
- Notice required by both parties
- The job title
- Any disciplinary rules relating to the job
- Grievance procedures.

A further requirement is that employers must issue on or before each pay day and for each employee an itemised statement showing:

- Gross wages/salary
- Net wages/salary
- Deductions and the reasons for them (unless these are a standard amount, in which case the reasons need only be repeated every 12 months)

● Details of part-payments, eg special overtime rates.

Unfair dismissal

One area where a distinction is made between the legislation applying to larger and small firms is in the sphere of unfair dismissal. Small, new firms cannot normally be sued for unfair dismissal by employees who have been on their payroll for less than two years; nor do they have to provide for post-maternity re-instatement if they have less than five employees and if re-instatement is impracticable. A further provision is that even if you do get caught out on the losing side of an unfair dismissal case, the tribunal is directed to take account of the size and resources of the firm in making an award.

Unfair dismissal cases have become less prevalent in the last few years, but it is still advisable to act reasonably if you do have to dismiss someone—and absolutely essential after they have been with you for the qualifying period. The law, incidentally, also extends to part-timers, if they work for you for more than 16 hours a week. There is no legislation on what is regarded by the industrial tribunal as 'reasonable behaviour' but the code of practice recommends that you should warn the employee in writing that you are dissatisfied with his conduct, warning him of the consequences if he fails to mend his ways and spell out what he is required to do to that end.

Incompetence, the most frequent cause of dismissal, is of course, difficult to express in writing because it is not quantifiable and the only thing one can say about it is that if you appoint someone who turns out to be incompetent you should dismiss them before the two qualifying years are up—however hard you might find it to do that to someone you otherwise like. Another, but more clear-cut cause of dismissal is persistent lateness or absenteeism, though there again, the advice would be to crack down on it in good time.

Redundancy

Redundancy, contrary to popular opinion, is not the same thing as dismissal but occurs when a job disappears and no one is brought in to replace the person who had been doing it. Again, employees become eligible for redundancy pay if they have been in a business for two years or more of continuous service. The employer can recover about half the money that has to be paid out from the Department of Employment, subject to a good deal of form filling. The sums involved in redundancy settlements are not large, but potential redundancy situations are something to look out for if you buy an existing business and take on their staff. You may find that you do not like some of the people the previous owner took on, or that you want to change or drop some of the things he was doing, with the result that staff will be made redundant. Irrespective of the fact that you did not hire the people concerned, you are still stuck with your responsibility towards them as their current employer, so that being the proverbial new broom can be a very costly exercise. Before buying a business, therefore, it is very important to look at the staff and at the extent of any redundancy payments or dismissals situations you could get involved in.

In the same context, another Act of Parliament you should keep an eye open for when buying a business is the Health and Safety at Work Act which lays down standards to which working premises have to conform. Before putting down your money you should check with the inspectors of the Health and Safety Executive that any premises you are buying or leasing meet those standards.

Pay as you earn (PAYE)

If you employ staff you will be responsible for deducting PAYE from their wages. The same applies to your own salary from a partnership or a limited company. The sums have to be paid monthly to the Inland Revenue by the employer.

You will receive from the tax office a tax deduction

card for each employee, with spaces for each week or month (depending on how they are paid) for the year ending 5 April. On these cards, weekly or monthly as the case may be, you will have to enter under a number of headings, details of tax, pay for each period and for the year to date. You will know how much tax to deduct by reading off the employee's tax code number, which has been allotted to him by the tax office, against a set of tables with which you will also be issued. Without going into technicalities, the way the tables work is to provide a mechanism, self-correcting for possible fluctuations of earnings, of assessing the amount of tax due on any particular wage or salary at any given point of the year.

At the end of the tax year you will have to make out two forms:

1. Form P60 issued to each employee. This gives details of pay and tax deducted during the year.
2. Form P35 for the Inland Revenue. This is a summary of tax and graduated National Insurance contributions for all employees during the year.

When an employee leaves, you should complete another form, P45, for him. Part of this form, showing his code number, pay and tax deducted for the year to date, is sent to the tax office. The other parts are to be handed by the employee to his new employer so that he can pick up the PAYE system where you left off.

Chapter 10
Advertising and Publicity

While some dealers swear that magazine and news-paper advertising brings in business and others that it is a waste of money, all seem to agree that the best form of promotion is personal recommendation. The proverbial grapevine is notoriously luxuriant in the antiques trade, and if you can build a reputation, not only for good stock at the right prices but also for friendliness and straight dealing, your customers will snowball. Maintaining good relations with your neighbouring dealers is important for similar reasons: they can often send their own clients on to you if they feel so disposed.

Editorial coverage of a business is also deemed to be a most valuable form of advertising. If you can persuade a newspaper or magazine to publish a story about you or your shop, or a specialist publication to illustrate an item from your stock, you can gain useful free publicity. Most well-established dealers are happy to supply photographs to journalists and authors in return for a credit line mentioning them in the publication concerned. While this hardly consti-tutes advertising, and its effect in drawing custom-ers is rarely measurable, the system provides a means of promoting the business and can be a useful 'flag-waving' exercise.

How much money you decide to spend on advertis-ing, if any, must be a personal matter and depend much on the nature of your business. You may take regular slots in magazines (rates are generally cheap-er if you book a series of advertisements), or you may try a single half or quarter page to see what sort of response it elicits, bearing in mind that regular advertising over a prolonged period is thought to be more fruitful. Some of the bigger dealers maintain that advertising is important to their prestige; they may spend thousands of pounds on whole pages of coloured advertising, and while direct response in terms of sales may be limited, it can be an important way of publicising the business.

Generally speaking, a pictorial advertisement is usually more successful than mere words, and prices can be a great help. Some committed advertisers who regularly illustrate items from stock with full descriptions reckon to sell most of them over the telephone. But apart from the measurable advantage of advertising a piece and selling as a direct result of the advertisement, you have to consider the value of publicising your name and your stock as a long-term investment.

On a less expensive level, you may find it useful to advertise in the small ads section of appropriate publications—either items 'for sale' or 'wanted'. These types of advertisement cost comparatively little and may be effective in eliciting a specific response.

When trade is buoyant and profits are good, some dealers spend money on advertising as a way of reducing their tax liability. In a sense this is another form of long-term investment as publicity gained during a good period for business can provide a cushion against a subsequent trough.

Promotions

Promoting your business can take many forms, ranging from small give-aways like pencils emblazoned with the firm's name to expensive private view parties, as well, of course, as the 'goodwill' type of promotion which is the result of personal recommendation and a reputation built up by word of mouth. The cost-effectiveness of direct promotion is difficult to evaluate and is probably a matter for well-established dealers, but many find that a special exhibition can give a lift to the business, both by providing a focus of interest for those organising it and, through the attention it attracts, by drawing potential new clients. Some picture dealers conduct their business entirely through a series of changing exhibitions, and while this may be hard work, it is certainly a way of keeping things lively and stimulating.

The acquisition of a suitable collection in its entirety, the publication of a book, the celebration of an anniversary, or simply the pursuit of a particular type of object over a period, can provide opportunities for exhibitions which will be a means of drawing attention to the business as a whole as well as buyers for the specific objects on view. Sometimes this will involve borrowing back from their present owners items sold in the past; it may mean 'putting by' objects and storing them over a considerable period, or paying an inflated price for something you really want. Publicising the exhibition and possibly holding an opening party for favoured individuals and the press can be expensive but is an important aspect of the exercise. The costs and problems involved must be weighed against the likely long-term advantages to the business.

Public relations

While everyone agrees that editorial coverage of an antiques business is of inestimable value in promoting it, many find that the assistance of a public relations consultant is all but essential in securing such publicity. For one thing, a good PR consultant should know the right people in the right places and be able to feed publicity material in directions where it is likely to elicit response and result in publication; for another, it is always easier for another person to blow your trumpet for you. If you tell people you are a good dealer with a shop full of fantastic stock, you are less likely to be taken seriously than if someone else says it for you. This is particularly true when dealing with the press.

The cost of hiring a PR consultant can be high, but it may be more cost-effective than widespread advertising. For instance, a London dealer mounting a specialised exhibition recently, hired a PR consultant to publicise it: through her selective but thrusting approach she succeeded in gaining editorial coverage for the exhibition in nearly 20 journals all over the world. It would have cost the dealer many times the PRO's fee to advertise in the same journals, and would probably have been less effective.

Public relations in the art world is a highly specialised business and there is only a small handful of consultants who make it their particular concern, but these few have sent many art and antique dealers to the peak of success. They have an immense number of journalistic and press contacts, built up over long periods, and can secure editorial space for their clients far more widely and effectively than any dealer would be able to do. In addition, they are valued by the press as sources of information, and this can be immeasurably helpful to dealers. For example, a non-specialist journalist wanting to write a feature about a particular aspect of art or antiques might go to one of these PR consultants for information. From her long experience she can give the names of dealers, or suggest places to visit (not necessarily her own clients) which are likely to be useful sources of copy.

As with advertising, continuity is held to be an important aspect of public relations. The success of a single well-publicised exhibition is likely to be diminished if it is not followed up, either by another exhibition, or by a different means of focusing attention on the dealer and his activities.

Antiques by mail order

Some dealers operate what amounts to a mail-order system of selling, alongside their shop-based business. They periodically compile catalogues of their stock, often illustrated with polaroid photographs, which they send to regular customers who will probably pay some sort of subscription for the service. Others, mainly specialists, make a habit of sending polaroid photographs to collector clients who they feel are likely to be interested in particular items. This specific form of promotion can be an especially useful way to maintain contact with clients from abroad.

Chapter 11
Company Stories

David Black: carpets and woven textiles

David Black specialises in carpets and woven textiles in his London gallery. From an initial outlay of £150 his stock value grew to about £250,000 in 15 years. But success has not come without effort and determination, and in his early years he had to weather setbacks that might have deterred a less enthusiastic dealer.

Trained as an advertising man, David had a strong interest in oriental carpets but only saw working with them as 'an impossible dream'—until 1964 that is. In that year a couple of friends offered him a half share in 30 carpets as a complement to the icon selling business they were setting up. He took the share for £150 and together they established themselves with four stalls in Portobello Road. Although his partners had more business experience than David, the venture did not prosper, probably because the overheads were too high. After six months David bought out his partners (for £200 over two years) and reduced the stall-holding to one.

As Portobello Road only operates on Friday afternoons and Saturdays, he spent the rest of the week doing odd jobs, mostly house-painting and carpentry, and did his buying in spare moments—nearly always from antique shops and the smaller auction rooms. In those days one could buy kilims (flatweaves) and Baluchi rugs quite cheaply because no dealers were interested in them. David found he could sell them quite successfully largely, he says, because he liked them himself and was able to communicate his own interest to his customers: this is always an important factor in the selling process.

114

Little by little his stock began to grow as he ploughed back his takings into the business. At the same time he was learning fast — 'There's nothing like putting your own money into something to learn about it' — and was getting to know the dealers.

Another six months later he managed to rent a derelict builder's store in what was then the seedy end of Ladbroke Grove. Over a two-month period he saved up for paint and light fittings, refurbished the building himself and proudly opened his new gallery in the afternoons. Nobody came in for five long weeks. Luckily he had kept on his Portobello Road stall and he still had odd jobs to do for bread and butter, otherwise he might have given up.

Eventually things began to move and the project seemed to be getting off the ground. Because the area was still what he calls 'heavy' — a few years later it became one of the most fashionable residential areas in London — he had difficulty in getting his gallery and stock insured. The inevitable happened: just as business seemed to be picking up he was burgled. Totally uninsured, he was cleaned out. At the time he had about £500-worth of other people's carpets in the gallery, and £300 of his own so he not only found himself without stock but also with considerable debts to pay off. Ironically, on the day of the break-in, the Commercial Union had agreed to take him on, on condition that he put in a burglar alarm.

Things seemed gloomy indeed, but David reckons that his burglary may have been a heavily disguised blessing. When he re-opened the shop after three months he found he'd earned himself a good deal of local sympathy; people from the immediate neighbourhood poured in and many of them spent money. However, it took him a good three years to clear his debts and recover from the burglary. In this period he was greatly helped by the support of other dealers, in particular Alexander Juran, who loaned him stock to sell on commission. Luckily, too, he had no family and he was able to continue his odd-jobbing in the mornings and open the shop during the afternoons. Most fortunately of all, it was a period when oriental carpets were becoming increasingly popular and he was able to tap a growing market.

At this stage he still didn't employ an accountant or run a bank loan (officially). There was no VAT to worry about in the 1960s and his business records were minimal. In 1967 Clive Loveless, an ex-journalist interested in carpets and out of a job, arrived on the scene and looked after the shop while David took a much-needed holiday. As Clive's knowledge and experience grew, it became clear that he and David had similar tastes if completely dissimilar personalities—one volatile and the other phlegmatic—and that they could work well together.

In 1972 they found themselves an accountant and a solicitor, drew up a legal partnership agreement and took out a bank loan. On the whole it has worked well. 'There's no equality in partnership,' says David, 'You have to settle for a great deal of give and take. Things tend to go well enough between partners when business is good, and when things are really bad you pull together beautifully.' It's when things are moderately bad that the most difficulties and resentments occur. But a partnership of some sort is essential, in David's view, especially for a specialist dealer who can be 'very much out on a limb'. Not only can a partner share the physical burdens of manning the shop (although they still open only in the afternoons) and finding stock, but he or she can act as a foil for the other.

Clive's journalistic experience has been invaluable in one aspect of the venture—the writing and publishing of books. Together they have now produced seven, filling the gaps they perceive in the literature on carpets, rugs, weavings and embroideries. Although their books tend to be expensive because they have comparatively short print runs, they have proved a commercial success, and David maintains this is simply because they fulfil an information need.

Sometimes the publication of a book has coincided with an exhibition—another way in which David Black exploits the full possibilities of his market. In discovering new fields, he says, 'you have to have very good footwork': in other words, you must be one

step ahead of the trend so that you are well into something when it becomes fashionable. Indeed, by writing books it is possible, at least in theory, to create
fashions. Among his future projects David intends to
devote a good deal of energy to the encouragement of
good modern carpet-making in areas of the Middle
East where the traditional skills have not died out.
At the same time he is moving into the field of traditional European textiles and weavings.

It is a source of some pride that within 15 years of
starting his business—with £150—David's stock is
worth around £250,000. His main problem now is
still capital: 'one's knowledge always grows faster
than one's purse,' and the prices of good quality carpets have leapt in recent years. David puts down a lot
of his success to luck, and says it must be the same
for most antique dealers, whatever their field. He is
sure that selling ability is as essential as good stock,
and finds that while he is better at selling to some of
their clients, Clive is more successful with others—
perhaps another argument in favour of partnerships.
They only buy what they like 'and we do have good
taste'—a vital factor in the carpet business, affirms
David.

One of the aspects of his business in which he takes
most pleasure is the restoration workshop. Four
people are employed and they undertake clients' carpet repairs as well as the restoration of damaged
pieces for the gallery. For David, it can be a highly
satisfactory form of rescue work. As a sideline he
undertakes valuations which he regards as a useful
(and not unprofitable) service for clients.

Although he belongs to both the BADA and
LAPADA, David regards their value as minimal:
'they live in a cocoon of unreality' and do little to further the cause of antiques or antique dealers. He has
scarcely more time for some of the auctioneers, many
of whose 'experts' apparently know next to nothing
and still collect high commissions.

Most of their customers are private individuals
who want to enjoy using carpets. David doesn't go
for the idea of 'collectors' with regard to carpets—
they are something to be lived with, not amassed. In

the past, foreign dealers from different countries have come in waves, influenced by the currency changes of the time, but at present most of their foreign trade is with private Americans rather than dealers. While much of their knowledge has come from books and from other dealers, David reckons to have learned an enormous amount from his customers, some of whom are extremely well-informed. It is this interest in carpets and their origins, beyond commercial considerations, which probably sets David Black apart from the general run of carpet dealers. He has built up a reputation not just for quality but for research, and for enthusiasm in sharing knowledge: whether he likes it or not, he is a true 'collector's dealer'.

During the two years since this book was first published, the partnership has been amicably dissolved and David Black is once more trading alone. His experimental ventures into the buying and selling of new but traditionally made carpets, especially from Turkey, have proved outstandingly successful, and have enabled him to survive the financial burden of buying out his partner.

Anne and Trevor Martin: furniture

Anne and Trevor Martin set up their own antiques business in Essex a little under two years ago. Their experiences must have been similar to those of other newcomers to the trade.

My wife and I have been trading as dealers for nearly two years and, as we expected for the early years, it has been a bumpy ride, partly because we have been learning, and partly because the market is still difficult. A difficult market is not necessarily a bad market: possibly, for the trade, the bad market was in the boom years up to 1980 when too much was sold too easily. The true antiques market must be about honesty and quality or it is nothing.

I decided to take early retirement from a career in international business so that my wife and I could work together while we still had time and energy enough to do so. We had both grown up with antique furniture and when we married 30 years ago we furnished our home with late Georgian and Victorian pieces, because they were then the cheapest furniture available to a hard-up couple. The idea of professional involvement was given more life some years ago when we were overcharged for a bad piece of upholstery and found that broken springs had been re-used. My wife began to take lessons and developed her skills within our home.

We were fortunate in being able to bring to our new venture some capital and business experience, as well as my wife's skills as an upholsterer. We are also fortunate in that our aesthetic tastes are similar and disagreements about style rarely arise. Above all, we had haunted antique shops and auction rooms all our married lives, and were not totally ignorant. We were lucky enough already to have a good accountant and an able and prompt solicitor. Anyone attempting a risk business on any serious scale must have professional support of this kind. Some people have the curious idea that antiques is a kind of fun business. In fact, like any other, it requires acceptance of a high percentage of routine drudgery and continuous hard work. An antiques enterprise must have a straightforward, efficient and effective business organisation behind it, whatever the scale. Only on these foundations can the aesthetic aspects, the fun part, rest.

The fact that we had some capital meant that setting up our own business did not involve selling or mortgaging the family home. My personal tax position was, oddly enough, helpful too. My last half year of full employment fell in the first half of a financial year and my already substantial tax payments were raised to a ridiculous figure by the 'handshake' I received for retiring early. This meant we had the second half of the tax year to get our business organised and to lay out our setting-up costs. By forming the business before I retired and by making it a sole proprietorship, its tax position became the same as my own, so setting up costs could be claimed against tax.

These activities were given a necessary reality in the tax man's eyes because trading also began. Although we made no active attempt to sell, people heard what we were up to and in the three months before we moved into our proper premises we sold over £3000-worth of furniture from a farmer's shed which we had rented. We had done this because we wanted to open with a comprehensive stock. Indeed, as soon as we had decided to move into the trade I raised a temporary overdraft from my bank (charges to be set against the business) and we began buying. We also decided that if our business was to prosper, turnover would have to exceed the level at which registration for VAT becomes necessary. Therefore, before buying any equipment for the business we sought VAT registration and for three VAT quarters our claims against purchases exceeded, quite substantially, our payments in regard to sales. The Customs and Excise rules specially provide for setting-up periods provided, of course, one does go on to trade on a reasonable scale.

At this stage I also set up the office, using my own study (tax allowable). Again, a substantial turnover meant having proper systems of stock control, invoicing and so on. Indeed, the VAT man has very rigorous requirements for an effective control and recording system, and the Inland Revenue require properly kept accounts if claims are to be made. If these are to be certified by an accountant then his professional status requires them to be of a high standard. Since we have been trading, we have often had cash offered 'in return for a discount'. We explain that cash makes no difference, as everything has to go through the books. I find keeping one set sufficiently arduous and, even if I wished to, am not clever enough to keep two sets or to do part of the trade on a cash basis as some are alleged to do.

Having no secretary for the first time in a quarter of a century (my wife, sensibly, has avoided typewriters all her life) the first essentials for the office were a typewriter and a photocopier. A portable electric typewriter goes a long way to concealing the unevenness of two-finger typing. A small copier is invaluable as a time-saver and for essential things like photocopying invoices for accounts records.

One requirement of the VAT people is sequentially numbered invoices. We decided it would cost little more to have these decently designed with our own house mark and to have similar stationery, cards and promotional literature. After all, if someone spends several hundred pounds with you they may well prefer something more than a receipt torn out of a 50p book. Dealers, and especially foreign dealers, require proper documents for Customs or VAT. We used the same colours and house sign for our van and shop. I was fortunate in knowing a good designer and printer from my business days in London.

Having mentioned the van it may be worth while to say we chose a Renault, having had good experiences from our Renault 4 (which we immediately put 'on the business'). The current range of Renault vans, Masters and Trafics, are excellent for the antiques trade as, being front-wheel drive, they have a very low loading platform and handle as easily as cars. We chose a diesel version for economy. We were fortunate in our timing as we were able to claim capital allowances on things like the photocopier and the van, but the 1984 Budget changed the rules.

While all these preparations were going on we were seeking the essential to any retail operation—a physical outlet. We had originally had the idea of running a 'warehouse' type operation rather than a conventional shop. Every time we found somewhere suitable the planners raised objections: 'not zoned', 'not enough parking', 'you may use the building for restoring but not for selling'... Apparently the 1947 Planning Act did not take into account the age-old tradition of the craftsman having his shop and workroom in the same premises.

In the end, we found a conventional shop in a town known as a centre of the antiques trade and large enough for our purposes. Most of our restoration work is done by 'outworkers' who operate from their own premises. Again, we were fortunate in being able to buy a freehold, albeit with the aid of a bank loan.

We looked at many leasehold properties, but they can cause great difficulties for small businesses. A 'full repairing lease' does not mean that you surrender the premises in the state in which you took them over, but fully repaired and decorated. Leases are nowadays short and subject to frequent 'upwards only' reviews: thus they can bring costs beyond your control and perhaps beyond the means of your business to support. Many people with little or no capital have no choice in this matter, but should get good advice first. A chartered surveyor can sometimes give a better steer than a lawyer.

Having been in a large organisation, I had been protected from many things like dealing with local bureaucracies. Since our venture into business on our own we have found private suppliers and services of all kinds invariably helpful and efficient. Our dealings with local authorities and the state corporations have been less happy. Regrettably, the norm seems to be inflexibility, dilatoriness, ignoring correspondence and blaming errors on the computer. We still await our refund from the Inland Revenue for the tax year before last and are having to pay for that money!

Customers are obviously among the most important considerations in setting up an antiques business. Whether one wants to sell mostly to other dealers, to exporters, to continental dealers, to collectors or to the public at large will determine the nature of the sales approach, choice of outlet, the stock itself and how it is advertised. It is also vital to decide early on whether you are going for high turnover with lower profit margins or high mark-ups with lower turnover. The quality of the goods you intend to sell obviously affects the margin you may seek to command. It is generally accepted in the antiques trade that the higher up market you go the more likely you are to succeed. The downward side leads to Steptoe and Son.

We have found that about 75 per cent of our sales are with private individuals looking for furniture they can use and enjoy in their homes. While a small proportion of our customers are dealers from abroad, the rest are British. Although a few of our clients like to do their own restoration, by and large they expect the goods they buy to be sound and in good repair. Chairs, in which we specialise, are subject to harder wear and tear than almost any other furniture, and restoration has to be a major consideration in our costings. The skill of the craftsmen we have met has been a great source of confidence to us. Within a 20-mile radius of countryside we have found polishers, veneerers, turners, joiners, upholsterers, rush and cane workers, ebonisers and carvers—in fact as rich a source of skills as ever was in the great days of English furniture making.

All in all we have had an interesting first year's trading and have covered our operating costs. We have met great friendliness in the trade and amongst most customers. No one has stolen anything (it might be different if we dealt in 'smalls') and we have had no dud cheques or bad debts. We have made errors, but so far no disastrous ones, and even after the two years since the project began, we do not think we would have done much differently, although we might wonder at the courage of innocence that set us on this course.

The lesson of the past two years (since this was written) has been that unit labour costs are the same for second-rate goods as they are for the best. We are therefore moving towards better quality stock with which we can make higher margins of profit on fewer sales. Like many others, we find that this more 'up-market' approach also gives us greater personal satisfaction.

Denzil and Nicky Grant: antiques and restoration

They combine furniture and textile restoration with antique dealing in their company, Suffolk Fine Arts Ltd, which trades as Denzil Grant Antiques, based at their home deep in the countryside. But it has not been all a bed of roses.

From an early age Denzil's gifts tended to be physical rather than academic: at school he was good at sport and good with his hands, but he was less good at passing exams. On leaving, he worked his way through an array of manual jobs before deciding he must learn a trade. An ability to work with wood and an interest in antiques set him on the path of furniture restoration. After gaining a City & Guilds certificate in cabinet-making he joined the furniture restoration course at West Dean College (see page 138) which he reckons is especially valuable in training finishers. While skill in furniture construction is not particularly hard to come by, the techniques of colouring and polishing old furniture are much more difficult to acquire, and he has found his grounding in these aspects of furniture restoration the most useful preparation for his subsequent experience.

While he was at West Dean he met his future wife, Nicky, a student of weaving and textile conservation. After leaving West Dean he spent a few rather demoralising months working for a local auctioneer in Suffolk where they live (Denzil found himself restoring and reproducing furniture for auction. He soon decided to set up his own restoration business. Things were not very easy at first, and he relied heavily on a handful of dealer clients, but expansion soon came in the form of a partnership with a Dutch businessman who was prepared to pay Denzil a commission for buying antiques (mostly oak furniture) and shipping them to Holland, restoring them first if necessary. Things began to look good, and Denzil's bank manager was impressed by the large sums of money on deposit, sent by the Dutchman in anticipation of Denzil's buying trips. Eventually they opened a shop near Bury St Edmunds, and another in Holland.

Inevitably, for these chance partnerships between comparative strangers are rarely successful in the long run, things began to go wrong. The Dutchman found himself over-committed and had to pull out of the partnership, leaving Denzil and Nicky with a large overdraft and a shop only half full of antiques.

Luckily the bank, clearly realising that the antiques were worth considerably less than the overdraft, decided not to declare the couple bankrupt. Although the experience was a less than happy one, compounded by the fact that Nicky was at that time extremely ill, Denzil had gained a great deal of knowledge and learned invaluable lessons about buying antiques at someone else's expense—a chance few are lucky enough to enjoy.

Since they have been on their own, and without a shop, Denzil has concentrated on the buying and restoring of furniture while Nicky spends most of her time cleaning and restoring woven and embroidered textiles, some of which she makes into cushions. At present she has enough work to keep her busy for a year or more, and could consider employing an assistant. They have a six year-old daughter who has adapted well to the pressures and irregularities of the antique dealer's life; although she is not yet old enough to join in and difficulties sometimes arise when both Nicky and Denzil need to go on buying trips or to fairs together, they can generally find friends or relations willing to look after her for odd days.

For the past five years their business has centred chiefly on a handful of major antiques fairs. These not only provide the main outlet for selling, but they are invaluable for building up contacts and giving a psychological impetus to both the restoration and dealing aspects of their work. Fairs mean intensive hard work and a high capital outlay, but most bring in good profits. They concentrate mainly on those fairs with an 1830 dateline for furniture, and although this can be limiting it does ensure a high standard.

Denzil drives between 40,000 and 50,000 miles a year in search of goods and reckons to cover virtually the whole country on his routes. Before a fair he will spend considerable time restoring any damaged pieces and making sure that everything is in tip top condition. As well as furniture he buys decorative items such as treen, metalwork and, of course, textiles, all of which must be 'right'. He knows he could make more money if he spread his net wider and was prepared to buy 'tat' but he would find this both ethically and aesthetically unsatisfactory. 'I am, after all, an antique dealer, not a purveyor of second-hand goods.' He buys only what he personally likes, and his profit margins when he sells vary enormously: he prefers to take a small profit on an item and sell it quickly rather than hold out for a high price. In this respect he recommends disregarding most accountants' advice to maintain a minimum percentage of profit. As far as the beginner is concerned, he says the most important thing is to *sell*, no matter how small the profit.

An ability to sell is a vital factor in success and, as Nicky says, this involves 'being a chameleon': you have to be able to gauge your customers and adapt your sales patter—if any—to their preferences. It is always easier to sell a piece that you yourself like. Denzil believes that success in selling has much to do with 'psyching up' one's image as an antique dealer. Whereas he knows his youth can be a disadvantage—older dealers are often unwilling to concede that anyone who has been in the business for less than a lifetime can know anything about anything—he is able to present himself as an energetic young enthusiast who gets the goods together and doesn't expect fancy profits. Running (see page 44) was one of the ways Denzil sold furniture when he first set up on his own, but he found it more often demoralising than enjoyable and now only does it 'if things get very sticky'.

At present he employs two assistants—a cabinet maker and a polisher—in his restoration workshop, and has recently moved and refurbished a historic barn which will become a permanent showroom next to their house. Both he and Nicky feel the need for a shop in a good high street site (preferably near other antique shops) but hope that the opening of the barn will be an improvement on their present situation where furniture for sale has to be viewed in overcrowded conditions in their own house. Most of their customers are from the trade and visit after making an appointment, but they do have some chance callers.

Like most successful antique dealers Denzil and Nicky maintain that good business foundations are of paramount importance. They employ an accountant but do their own VAT returns, and, most important of all, they keep up a daily balance record which enables them to know at any time, down to the last penny, how things are going. Denzil is sure that more dealers are undermined by failure to keep precise and frequent records of their business dealings than by any other factor. He recommends taking out the biggest overdraft the bank will allow, and in this regard he feels that his period of partnership with the Dutch businessman helped him considerably.

In spite of the ups and down of the antiques trade in general, and of their own experiences in particular, Nicky and Denzil thrive on the commitment and the 'self-imposed discipline' of dealing only in 'right' goods, and buying and restoring according to the strictest standards of aesthetic judgement.

Nearly two years ago Denzil acquired the lease of a two-storey shop in Long Melford and has since been able to add workshop and warehouse premises (shared with a partner) at the back. This has given them the 'high street' base they needed and, with the fairs in which they continue to participate, the business has grown substantially during the past two years.

Michael Wisehall: furniture and decorative objects

Michael Wisehall has been interested in antiques for as long as he can remember. He stocks eighteenth- and nineteenth-century furniture and all kinds of decorative objects in his medium-sized shop at Knutsford in Cheshire, and enjoys being an 'old-fashioned' dealer.

After leaving school in 1965 Michael went to work for a dealer in Knutsford who also allowed him to sell some of his own goods from the shop. Within two years he had started a business of his own on the proceeds of his sales and with the help of a few hundred pounds in savings.

His early stock consisted largely of shipping goods, but he says the same stock would now be rated as antiques of highly respectable quality and would most likely sell on the home market. At that stage the American and Italian trades were very strong and he did a good deal of export business, but by 1970 his instincts drew him away from the over-commercial 'shipping rat race' and into a more gentle way of dealing. His business is now concerned largely with members of the British trade and he tries to encourage more and more private customers.

In 1973, at the age of 24, he was admitted to the BADA and he has found this a great help to his business, mainly for the prestige it brings—he is one of the very few BADA dealers in the north of England; it also involves him in valuations, shipping assessments and other advisory matters. In 1983 he was elected to the BADA Council.

Michael buys carefully, and only what he likes; quality is much more important to him than age, and he has a particular interest in late nineteenth-century 'progressive' furniture. He travels all over the country to buy stock—and finding the right goods is getting more and more difficult—but he rarely buys in London and almost never at auction: 'I can do 20 shops in the time it takes to view a sale,' and anyway he dislikes the 'political' elements that tend to creep into the auction world.

Much more of his time is spent out buying than in the shop, and he relies heavily on his full-time manager, who has worked for him for ten years. Down the road he has a restoration workshop where he employs a full-time cabinet-maker for straightforward repairs and finishing; for specialist jobs like leathering, metal restoration, textile conservation and so on, he calls upon other craftsmen, mostly in London.

He used to participate in antiques fairs but has given them up since he finds the datelines too restricting, and at the same time feels that fairs can dictate trade too much: 'People go into limbo waiting for their next fair, and seem to abandon the day-to-day business of dealing from a shop.'

Michael likes to keep his stock moving and is prepared to take a lower profit in return for a high turnover. The shop display is very important in this respect, he says, and it helps morale enormously to change things round often. During the recent recession he largely managed to avoid the stagnation and boredom which has a correspondingly depressing effect on customers, by changing the shop around frequently, and keeping everything dusted and polished. Even if sales were down, things looked fresh and interesting.

The psychology of dealing is most important, he maintains, and salesmanship is 'a matter of finding the right level between pushiness and disinterest'. He aims to make people feel at ease in his shop, and he thinks the communication of his own interest in his stock plays a vital part in selling.

He would recommend anyone wanting to start an antiques business to open a shop at the outset if possible. One-day fairs and markets are all very well, he says, but they rarely lead beyond that level. If a shop is a financial impossibility to begin with, working for a good general dealer is probably the next best way to begin.

Appendix

National telephone dialling codes are given in the address lists, though local codes may differ.

Courses

Degree courses

Although this list is not exhaustive, it covers most of the history of art courses offered in British universities and polytechnics.

Most history of art courses require at least two and often three A level GCE passes, and the value of European languages at both O and A level is emphasised again and again; nearly all courses require students to have, or to acquire a reading knowledge of at least one European language. After languages, history of art, history, art and English are among the favoured subjects, but sciences are considered useful by several universities.

Gallery and museum visits constitute an important aspect of nearly every degree course and many include a period of study abroad.

Brighton Polytechnic
Moulsecoomb, Brighton, East Sussex BN2 4AT;
0273 604141
BA(Hons) degree course in history of design.

Courtauld Institute of Art
20 Portman Square, London W1H 0BE;
01-935 9292

1. Three-year degree course leading to BA(Hons) in the history of art.
2. Postgraduate courses and studies leading to MA, MPhil, PhD or DLit.

3. Three-year diploma course in the conservation of paintings.
4. Diploma in the conservation of textiles. A three-year course based at the Textile Conservation Centre at Hampton Court Palace.
5. Two-year MA course in the history of dress.

Edinburgh University
Faculty of Arts Office, David Hume Tower, George Square, Edinburgh EH8 9JX; 031-667 1011

1. MA(Hons) in history of art.
2. MA(Hons) in fine art (a combined course in practical art and art history which lasts five years).
3. History of art may also be taken as part of the MA (General) degree, as part of a joint MA(Hons) in history of art and Italian, or MA(Hons) in history of art and French.

North Staffordshire Polytechnic
College Road, Stoke-on-Trent ST4 2DE; 0782 45531
BA(Hons) course in history of design and the visual arts.

Sheffield City Polytechnic
Pond Street, Sheffield S1 1WB; 0742 20911
BA(Hons) course in the history of art, design and film, with a bias towards the twentieth century.

University of Aberdeen
Regent Walk, Aberdeen AB9 1FX; 0224 40241
Ordinary MA and Honours degree courses in the history of art.

University of Bristol
Senate House, Tyndall Avenue, Bristol BS8 1TH; 0272 303030
History of art may be taken as a subsidiary subject for BA(Hons) degrees in arts subjects.

University of Cambridge
University Registry, Old Schools, Cambridge CB2 1TN; 0223 358933

The history of art tripos (course) covers the
history, criticism and theory of architecture and
the figurative arts. It may only be taken after
Part 1 of another tripos, and so constitutes only
a proportion of a BA degree course.

University College
London, Gower Street, London WC1E 6BT;
01-387 7050
Three-year BA(Hons) degree courses in: history
of art (with history or philosophy); English and
history of art; French and history of art; German
and history of art; history and history of art;
Italian and history of art; and philosophy and
history of art. History of art is also included in
the syllabus for the mainly practical four-year
BA course in fine art at the Slade School of Fine
Art.

University of East Anglia
Norwich NR4 7TJ; 0603 56161

1. BA(Hons) degree in history of art and
   architecture.
2. A one-year postgraduate MA course in
   advanced art-historical studies, and MPhil and
   PhD degrees are also offered to suitably
   qualified graduates.

University of Essex
Wivenhoe Park, Colchester, Essex CO4 3SQ;
0206 862286

1. A BA degree scheme in art history and theory,
   and joint degree schemes in literature and art,
   and philosophy and art.
2. Various one-year MA schemes in art history
   and theory.

University of Leeds
Leeds LS2 9JT; 0532 31751

1. Four-year course leading to BA(Hons) in
   history of the fine and the decorative arts.
2. Four-year course leading to BA(Hons) in fine
   art. Combines practical work with the history
   of art.

3. Three-year BA(Hons) course in history of art.
4. Two-subject BA(Hons) courses. Combine history of art with English, German, history of scientific thought, music, Italian, religious studies, sociology, Spanish, theology or philosophy.

University of Leicester
Leicester LE1 7RH; 0533 554455

1. History of art is the main element in a three-year BA degree course which includes other subjects, notably languages or history.
2. History of art may form a smaller part of a combined studies degree.

University of London Extra-mural Department
26 Russell Square, London WC1B 5DQ; 01-636 8000
A variety of part-time degree courses is offered.

University of Manchester
Manchester M13 9PL; 061-273 3333
Three-year BA(Hons) course in history of art.

University of Nottingham
Nottingham NG7 2RD; 0602 56101
Art history may be taken for single Honours or for joint Honours with English or German.

University of Reading
Whiteknights, Reading RG6 2AH; 0734 875123

1. Four-year course in art and history of art leading to BA(Hons).
2. Three-year BA(Hons) course in history of art and architecture.
3. Three- and four-year combined subjects degree (BA) courses in history of art with English, French, German or Italian.

University of St Andrews
Fife, Scotland KY16 9AL; 0334 76161
Single Honours degrees in art history, or joint

133

degrees with a wide range of subjects are offered.
The courses cover painting, sculpture,
architecture, the graphic and applied arts, in
their historical context and from a strongly
visual angle.

PhD, MLitt, MPhil and diploma in art history
courses are also available.

University of Stirling
Stirling FK9 4LA; 0786 3171
General degree course in the history of fine
art.

University of Sussex
Falmer, Brighton BN1 9RH; 0273 606755
BA(Hons) courses in history of art are offered in
the School of Cultural and Community Studies
(three years), in the School of English and
American Studies (three years) and in the School
of European Studies (four years).

University of Warwick
Coventry CV4 7AL; 0203 24011
Three-year first degree course in history of art.
Covers painting, architecture and sculpture;
German and Italian are part of the syllabus,
and one term is spent in Venice.

Victoria and Albert Museum/
Royal College of Art
Department of Cultural History,
Royal College of Art, Kensington Gore,
London SW7; 01-584 5020
A two-year postgraduate course in 'design and
decorative arts: history and technique' leading to
an MA.

Westfield College
Kidderpore Avenue, Hampstead,
London NW3 7ST; 01-435 7141
Three-year BA(Hons) courses in history of art
(with history), and combined studies in history of
art with German or Spanish (compare with
University College, London).

Conservation and restoration courses

Association of British Picture Restorers
Station Avenue, Kew, Richmond,
Surrey TW9 3QA; 01-948 5644
Five-year apprenticeships in conservation and
restoration of paintings, leading to full
membership of the ABPR.

Camberwell School of Art and Crafts
Peckham Road, London SE5 8UF; 01-703 0987

1. Two-year diploma and two-year higher diploma
   for paper conservation.
2. Three-year diploma course in print and
   drawing restoration.

Cambridge University
Hamilton-Kerr Institute, Whittlesford,
Cambridge CB2 4NE; 0223 832040
Three- or four-year course for graduates, in
conservation of paintings, leading to certificate.

City and Guilds of London Art School
124 Kennington Park Road, London SE11;
01-735 2306
Three-year diploma course in conservation of
wood, stone and allied materials.

Colchester Institute
School of Printing, Sheepen Road, Colchester,
Essex CO3 3LL; 0206 570271
Two-year diploma course in book conservation.

**Council for Small Industries in Rural Areas
(CoSIRA)**
141 Castle Street, Salisbury, Wiltshire SP1 1EX;
0722 336255
Various sandwich-type courses in furniture-
making, antique restoration, wood-turning and
upholstery.

Courtauld Institute of Art
20 Portman Square, London W1H 0BE;
01-935 9292
(see Degree courses, page 130 and Tate Gallery,
page 138).

Gateshead Technical College
Durham Road, Gateshead NE9 5BN;
0632 770524

1. Two-year diploma course in conservation of watercolours, prints and drawings.
2. Two-year diploma course in conservation of paintings.

Guildford County College of Technology
Stoke Park, Guildford, Surrey GU1 1EZ;
0483 31251
Two-year diploma course in bookbinding and book restoration.

Hackney College
Hackney Centre, Dalston Lane, London E8 1LJ;
01-985 8484
Two-year courses in horology leading to the diploma in technical horology and the British Institute of Horology certificate.

International Centre for the Study of the Preservation and the Restoration of Cultural Property (ICCROM)
Via San Michele 13, 00153 Rome, Italy
The international body of conservators and restorers runs a number of courses at its Rome headquarters for those already specialising in some aspect of conservation.

1. Six-month course in architectural conservation.
2. Four-month course in conservation of mural paintings.
3. Four-month course in scientific principles of conservation.
4. Eighteen-day course on preventive conservation in museums.

London College of Furniture
41-71 Commercial Road, London E1 1LA;
01-247 1953
Two-year diploma courses in cabinet-making and furniture technology.

London College of Printing
Processes Department, Elephant and Castle,
London SE1 6SB; 01-735 8484
Thirty-week, part-time courses in book and
document conservation.

National Maritime Museum
Greenwich, London SE10 9NF; 01-858 4422
Four-year diploma course in conservation of
fine or applied art.

Robin Hood's Workshop
18 Bourne Street, London SW1; 01-730 0425
Ten-week, part-time courses in repair and
restoration of china, for beginners.

Royal School of Needlework
25 Princes Gate, London SW7 1QE; 01-589 0077
Two-year course in embroidery conservation—
for those with proven aptitude.

Rycotewood College
Thame, Oxfordshire; 084421 2501

1. Two-year, full-time diploma course in fine
   craftsmanship and design which includes
   furniture restoration.
2. One-year, full-time certificate course in fine
   craftsmanship and design for mature students
   and those with previous experience.
3. One-year, full-time course leading to the higher
   certificate in fine craftsmanship and design—
   for students with a good grounding in craft
   skills who want to specialise.

Society of Archivists
Conservation Training Scheme,
West Yorkshire Record Office, Deeds Registry,
Newstead Road, Wakefield WF1 2DE;
0924 367111
Two-year course in archive conservation leading
to the certificate; open only to those already
employed in the field.

Southampton College of Higher Education
East Park Terrace, Southampton SO9 4WW;
0703 29381

Four-year, one-day-a-week course in book
conservation, leading to a certificate.

The Tate Gallery
Conservation Department, Millbank,
London SW1P 4RG; 01-821 1313
Four-year conservation course in easel paintings
and modern art, leading to the Courtauld
Institute and Tate Gallery diploma in
conservation—for graduates.

Textile Conservation Centre
Apartment 22, Hampton Court Palace,
East Molesey, Surrey KT8 9AU;
01-943 0723

1. A comprehensive three-year postgraduate
   course in textile conservation, run in
   conjunction with the Courtauld Institute
   of Art.
2. In-service training courses for tapestry
   and rug conservation and for fabric-
   covered objects, including upholstered
   furniture.

Victoria and Albert Museum
South Kensington, London SW7 2RL;
01-589 6371
Four-year diploma course in conservation of
fine or decorative arts—for graduates.

West Dean College
West Dean, Chichester, West Sussex PO18 0QZ;
024363 301

1. One- and two-year professional courses in the
   restoration of antique furniture, established by
   the BADA in 1972.
2. One- and two-year courses in the restoration of
   antique clocks, designed for those with
   previous horological experience and/or
   engineering and metalworking skills.
3. One- and two-year professional courses in
   antique ceramic and porcelain restoration,
   open to anyone over 18 who is skilled with
   tools and materials (experience in pottery-

modelling, drawing and decoration is helpful)
and who is keenly interested in antique
ceramics.
4. West Dean also offers a wide range of short
(seven-day, five-day, four-day, three-day and
weekend) courses in antique and craft subjects,
suitable for beginners, enthusiasts or simply
for 'appetite-whetting'.

General courses

Christie's fine arts course
63 Old Brompton Road, London SW7 3JS;
01-581 3933
Three-term course designed to give a firm and
practical grounding in the fine and decorative
arts of the western world, ie painting, sculpture,
domestic architecture, furniture, ceramics, glass,
metalwork and textiles.

Fine Art Tutors
85 Belsize Park Gardens, London NW3;
01-586 0312
One-year courses in the history of European art.

Gemmological Association of Great Britain
Saint Dunstan's House, Carey Lane,
London EC2; 01-726 4374
Two-year, part-time courses which may be done
by correspondence with occasional tutorial
sessions or at college classes, leading to the
Association's diploma and Fellowship.

Geoffrey Godden
17 Crescent Road, Worthing, Sussex; 0903 35958
Short non-residential courses on various aspects
of ceramics.

Inchbald School of Design
7 Eaton Gate, London SW1; 01-730 5508

1. One-year fine and decorative arts course.
2. Ten-week course in the fine and decorative
   arts—actually a single term of the one-year
   course, for those who cannot attend during a
   whole year.

3. Eight-week course in the development of interior design, 1700-1983.

Modern Art Studies
140 Sloane Street, London SW1X 9AY; 01-730 5608
A three-term course on the history of modern art, 1848 to the present day. Classes are held three mornings each week at the Institute of Contemporary Art.

New Academy for Art Studies
3 Albion Street, London W2; 01-262 5462
Three-term course covering the fine and decorative arts for 'school leavers, university graduates and mature students'.

Sotheby's
30 Oxford Street, London W1R 1RE;
01-408 1100
Three-month courses in: Styles in Art, to introduce students to the stylistic developments in European fine and decorative arts from classical antiquity to the present; Seventeenth- and Eighteenth-Century Decorative Art; Nineteenth and Twentieth-Century Decorative Art; a study tour in England or abroad is an optional supplement.
All courses are closely linked with Sotheby's and the art auction business.
Works of Art Course: a three-term course on the fine and decorative arts.

Study Centre for the History of the Fine and Decorative Arts
9 Westwood Gardens, London SW13 0LB;
01-846 9224

1. Highly regarded one-year diploma course in the fine and decorative arts based at the Victoria and Albert Museum.
2. A ten-week decorative arts course for 20 students, covering a similar syllabus to that of the diploma students in their second term, but with historical and architectural background included.

Packers and shippers

**Alltransport International Group Ltd &
Vulcan Freight Services Ltd**
Unitair Centre, Great South West Road,
Feltham, Middlesex TW14 8NT;
01-751 3101

Anglo-American Shipping Co Ltd
School Close, Burgess Hill,
West Sussex RH15 9RX; 04446 45928

Blatchpack Robinson
22-4 Smyth Road, Ashton, Bristol;
0272 665996

James Bourlet
3 Space Waye, Feltham, Middlesex;
01-751 1155

British Antique Exporters Ltd
Queen Elizabeth Avenue, Burgess Hill,
West Sussex RH15 9RX; 04446 45577

Davies Turner
334 Queenstown Road, London SW8 4NG;
01-622 9361

C R Fenton
Beachy Road, Old Ford, London E3 2NX;
01-533 2711

Gander & White Shipping Ltd
21 Lillie Road, London SW6 1TT; 01-381 0571

Hedleys Humpers Ltd
157-9 Iverson Road, London NW6; 01-624 6874

Lou Lewis,
Unit T, Avis Way Industrial Estate, Newhaven,
East Sussex BN9 0EN; 07912 3901

Lockson Services Ltd
29 Broomfield Street, London E14; 01-515 8600

London and Southern Shipping Ltd
14 Clifton Hill, Brighton BN1 3HQ;
0273 202989

Masterpack Ltd
Albion House, 860 Coronation Road,
London NW10; 01-961 1222

Stephen Morris Shipping Ltd
89 Upper Street, London N1; 01-354 1212

Pitt & Scott Ltd
20-24 Eden Grove, London N7 8ED;
01-607 7321

L J Roberton Ltd
Marlborough House, Cooks Road,
London E15 2PW; 01-519 2020

W B Airfreight Ltd
69-70G Building 521, Cargo Terminal,
London Airport, Heathrow; 01-897 2551

Wingate & Johnson (Fine Art) Ltd
78 Broadway, London E15 1NG; 01-555 8123

Public relations consultants

Sue Bond
46 Greswell Street, London SW6 6PP;
01-381 1324

Heather McConnell Public Relations
18 St George Street, London W1R 9DE;
01-493 6420

Jill Thornton
Thornton Associates, 27 Henniker Mews,
London SW3 6BL; 01-351 5242

Other useful addresses

**Advisory, Conciliation and Arbitration Service
(ACAS)**
Head Office, Almack House, 26 King Street,
London SW1Y 6QW; 01-214 6000

Alliance of Small Firms and Self-Employed People
42 Vine Road, East Molesey, Surrey KT8 9LF;
01-979 2293

Antiquarian Booksellers Association
Suite 2, 26 Charing Cross Road,
London WC2H 0DG; 01-379 3041

Arts Council of Great Britain
105 Piccadilly, London W1V 0AU; 01-629 9495

Association of British Picture Restorers
Station Avenue, Kew, Richmond,
Surrey TW9 3QA; 01-948 5644

British Antique Dealers' Association
20 Rutland Gate, London SW7 1BD; 01-589 4128

British Hallmarking Council
PO Box 47, Birmingham B3 2RP; 021-236 9021

British Horological Institute
Upton Hall, Upton, Newark,
Nottinghamshire NG23 5TE; 0636 813795

British Insurance Brokers Association
Fountain House, 130 Fenchurch Street,
London EC3M 5DJ; 01-623 9043

**CINOA (Confédération Internationale des
Négociants en Oeuvres d'Art)**
The International Art Dealers' Association,
54 Boulevard de Waterloo, 1000 Brussels,
Belgium

Companies House
55-71 City Road, London EC1 1BB; 01-253 9393

**Council for Small Industries in Rural Areas
(CoSIRA)**
141 Castle Street, Salisbury, Wiltshire SP1 3TP;
0722 336255

Department of Trade and Industry
Export Licensing Branch
Millbank Tower, Millbank, London SW1P 4QU;
01-211 6611

Small Firms Division
Ashdown House, 127 Victoria Street,
London SW1E 6RB; 01-212 8667, 8721, 6206

143

For regional offices, dial 100 and ask for freefone 2444.

Fire Protection Association
Aldermary House, Queen Street, London EC4; 01-248 5222

Guild of Master Craftsmen
170 High Street, Lewes, East Sussex; 07916 77374

HM Customs and Excise
VAT Administration Directorate, King's Beam House, Mark Lane, London EC3R 7HE; 01-283 8911

HM Stationery Office
Atlantic House, Holborn Viaduct, London EC1P 1BN; mail order 01-622 3316

Incorporated Society of Valuers and Auctioneers
3 Cadogan Gate, London SW1; 01-235 2282

Joint Credit Card Companies
General Sales Office, 30-31 Newman Street, London W1P 4LJ; 01-323 2861

London and Provincial Antique Dealers' Association
3 Cheval Place, London SW7 1EW; 01-584 7911

Professional Data Management
The Studio, 79 Falcon Road, London SW11 2PF

Registrar of Companies
Companies House, Crown Way, Maindy, Cardiff CF4 3UZ; 0222 388588

120 Bothwell Street, Glasgow G2 7JP; 041-248 2700

102 Telford Road, Edinburgh EH4 2NP; 031-343 1911

Royal Institution of Chartered Surveyors
12 Great George Street, London SW1; 01-222 7000

Society of Fine Art Auctioneers
7 Blenheim Street, London W1Y 0AS;
01-629 2933

Society of London Art Dealers
148 New Bond Street, London W1Y 0JT

Further reading

British Art & Antiques Yearbook (National
Magazine Company)

Careers in Antiques, Noël Riley (Kogan Page)

The Complete Guide to London's Antique Markets,
Jeremy Cooper (Thames and Hudson)

Consumer Law for the Small Business, Patricia
Clayton (Kogan Page)

*Croner's Reference Book for the Self-employed and
Smaller Business* (Croner Publications)

Financial Management for the Small Business,
Colin Barrow (Kogan Page)

The Guardian Guide to Running a Small Business,
5th edn, ed Clive Woodcock (Kogan Page)

Guide to the Antique Shops of Britain (Antique
Collectors Club)

How to Buy a Business, Peter Farrell (Kogan Page)

*Law for the Small Business, The Daily Telegraph
Guide*, 4th edn, Patricia Clayton (Kogan Page)

*Working for Yourself: the Daily Telegraph Guide to
Self-employment*, 8th edn, Godfrey Golzen
(Kogan Page)

Periodicals
Antique Collecting, 5 Church Street, Woodbridge,
Suffolk

Antique Collector, National Magazine Co,
72 Broadwick Street, London W1V 2BP

Antique Dealer & Collectors Guide, IPC Magazines,
King's Reach Tower, Stamford Street,
London SE1 9LS

Antique Furniture & Art Weekly Bulletin,
HP Publishing, 226 Court Oak Road, Harborne,
Birmingham B32 2EG

Apollo, Minster House, Arthur Street,
London EC4R 9AX

Art & Antiques (American) 89 Fifth Avenue,
New York, NY 10003, USA

The Burlington Magazine, Elm House,
10-16 Elm Street, London WC1X 0BP

Clique (weekly on antiquarian books),
75 World's End Road, Handsworth Wood,
Birmingham B20 2NS

Collectors World, Frank Allan Publishing,
Chesham Close, Cedar Road, Romford,
Essex RM7 7EY

The Connoisseur, Hearst Corporation,
National Magazine House, 72 Broadwick Street,
London W1V 2BP

Country Life, IPC Magazines, King's Reach Tower,
Stamford Street, London SE1 9LS

Hali (quarterly on oriental carpets and textiles),
193A Shirland Road, London W9 2EU

International Toy and Doll Collector,
Alton House, Alton Street, Ross-on-Wye,
Herefordshire

Period Home, Period Home Publications,
Caxton House, High Street, Tenterden,
Kent TN30 6BD

Index

Financial Management for the Small business

The *Daily Telegraph* Guide
Colin Barrow

It is claimed that 70% of new businesses fail in their first year; the problem is usually financial. This book is a practical guide to controlling finance and improving business performance. It sets out to demonstrate how financial controls can be used to manage the money in the business on a day-to-day basis.

Colin Barrow is also co-author of **Taking Up a Franchise**

Contents

Paperback ISBN 0 85038 751 5
Hardback ISBN 0 85038 750 7
240 pages, 216x138mm

Consumer Law for the Small Business

Patricia Clayton

The first comprehensive guide to consumer law written specifically for the small businessman, this book gives detailed practical advice on such subjects as:

*Consumer credit
*Competition and fair trading
*Consumer safety
*The supply of goods and services
*Pricing
*Misrepresentation

Patricia Clayton is a solicitor and barrister. She lectures and writes on business law, and is in practice as a solicitor in London. She is the author of **Law for the Small Business,** also published by Kogan Page.

Paperback ISBN 085038 648 9
Hardback ISBN 0 85038 618 7
160 pages, 216x138mm

Law for the Small Business
Fourth Edition
The *Daily Telegraph* Guide
Patricia Clayton

Law for the Small Business covers every aspect of the law affecting the small business, explaining how to start a business, how to keep it going and how to avoid all the legal pitfalls. Each subject is treated clearly and succinctly, providing in one volume a complete reference guide. This new edition has been revised and updated to include recent legislation.

Contents
Preface

1. **Starting out: sole trader, partnership or company**
2. **Establishing the business**
3. **Capital and profits**
4. **Running the business**
5. **Premises**
6. **Taxation**
7. **Insurance**
8. **Employment law**
9. **Trading**
10. **Cash and credit at home and abroad**
11. **Intellectual property: patents, copyrights and trademarks**
12. **Litigation**
13. **Collecting your debts**
14. **Bankruptcy and mergers**
15. **Takeovers and mergers**

Patricia Clayton is a solicitor and barrister. She lectures and writes on business law, and is in practice as a solicitor. She is also the author of **Consumer Law for the Small business.**

Hardback ISBN 0 85038 893 7
Paperback ISBN 0 85038 894 5
286 pages, 216x138mm

Working for Yourself

Eighth Edition

The *Daily Telegraph* Guide to Self-Employment

Godfrey Golzen

This best-selling book will help you turn the dream of working for yourself into reality. It provides a clear, straightforward account of how to make a success of self-employment and surveys many of the opportunities available.

*Raising capital
*Seeking professional advice
*Running a part-time business
*Marketing your product
*Employing people
*Accounting and taxation
*Pensions for the self-employed
*Exporting

Contents

'a good investment before taking the plunge'
THE NORTHERN ECHO
'essential reading' **BRITISH BUSINESS**
'one of the best, if not the best, book on going into business' **FIRST VOICE**

ISBN 1 85091 074 X
312 pages, 216x138mm

How to Buy a Business
The *Daily Telegraph* Guide
Peter Farrell

*Judging the track record
*Why and when should you buy?
*Evaluating the assets
*What is the right price?
*Can you afford it?
*Paying for it

The author discusses all these problems and points out the advantages and the risks.

Peter Farrell writes extensively on business and money subjects and his other books include **Spare-time Income.**

Paperback ISBN 0 85038 635 7
Hardback ISBN 0 85038 634 9
160 pages, 216x138mm

Successful Expansion for the Small Business

The *Daily Telegraph* Guide

M J Morris

Badly thought-out expansion can easily cause the failure of a firm. Because most small firm owners personally guarantee their firm's debts, business failure can mean personal ruin. This book aims to guide owners through the pitfalls and towards expanding on sound foundations. Topics covered include:

*Managing people properly
*Strategic planning for results
*Ways in which to expand
*Control of the growing firm
*Finance
*Using advisers
*Marketing
*Production
*Law

Contents

Foreword by David Davenport, Chairman of CoSIRA

Paperback ISBN 0 85038 823 6
Hardback ISBN 0 85038 822 8
160 pages, 216x1388mm